DAILY STAR

First Book of

SEXUAL

QUESTIONS
&
ANSWERS

by

CHRISTINE WEBBER

To my lovely husband, David Delvin,
who answers all my questions!

Special thanks to my agent, Chris Green, for her unflagging support and to Sue Bailey and Nigel Blundell for their encouragement. Also to my BRILLIANT researcher, Hazel Spokes.

This edition published 1994 by Sunburst Books, Deacon House, 65 Old Church Street, London SW3 5BS

ISBN 1 85778 069 8
Printed and bound in the United Kingdom

DAILY STAR

First Book of

SEXUAL
QUESTIONS
&
ANSWERS

CONTENTS

Introduction

Welcome to the first of my books on sexual questions, which have been taken from my column in the *Daily Star* newspaper.

Sex not only keeps the human race going, but it's also a vital part of most peoples' lives. They may hate sex, they may love it. They may long to do it with someone they're not married to, or with someone of the same sex. They may dream of making it more exciting, or wonder whether they're ever going to get any sex at all! But one thing is clear, very few folk are indifferent to it.

People are always asking us agony aunts whether we make up the more bizarre questions on our pages! They seem to believe that some of the more outrageous offerings must be the product of a vivid imagination. But I can assure you, these strange things do happen. So there's no need for me to be creative. My readers' queries provide all the material I need.

Although people write in on all manner of topics, sex, not surprisingly, is the most popular. But men and women worry about different things. Blokes are particularly bothered about dimensions and performance, while women are usually more anxious about emotions. But at the end of the day, both sexes want the same things - love and security.

On the way to finding these, it's true that plenty of folk do a lot of weird and crazy things - they sometimes "do" plenty of wrong people too - wrong for them, that is. You see, what I've learned doing this job is that most people ultimately want the happiness that only a good relationship can bring. They want to wake up glad to be beside their loved one and they want to look forward to turning the key in the lock of their front door at the end of the day, knowing that the person they care for most will be there.

But even great relationships have to be worked at. And talking together about feelings, hopes, desires AND sex can help enormously. In fact when a couple CAN'T talk about such things they're usually in deep trouble.

I believe that most folk are kind, decent, generous and loving. They want a monogamous relationship, but one that is stimulating and fulfilling. They also want to iron out small difficulties before they become larger. This book - which is funny, sad, weird and saucy all at the same time - should help you to achieve this.

I hope that people will read it and realise that their problems are not unusual. And if it gets couples talking together about things they've never discussed before, that'll be great.

Christine Webber

Relationship Problems

Where does sex for its own sake stop and a relationship begin?

That's a difficult question for many men. For women the relationship has sometimes been going on in their mind before the first kiss!

Very few people have explosive sex with strangers, though some would claim that they have. For most of us, sex gets better and better the more we know and care for someone. We also get to know what turns on our partners in bed. Unless you're psychic, this rarely happens on a first date.

But once you care for someone and have a long term romance, or even live with them or marry, your relationship may face difficulties at some time or another. This section contains a wide selection of common problems.

Q. I'm a girl of 18 and I've met this fantastic man. He comes into the chemist's shop where I work - usually to buy after-shave and condoms. I was amazed when he asked me out, as he's 45. But I went, as I'd never met anyone like him before.

He's got a brilliant flat, like something out of a film. There are mirrors everywhere and furry rugs on the floor. I went to bed with him the first night I went out with him. I couldn't help myself. And he's marvellous at it! He does lots of different things and he has a drawer full of sex gadgets that really blow my mind.

The trouble is that my old friends seem boring next to him and I spend all my time just longing for our next meeting.

He has other women, but he has told me that he considers girls who get jealous to be pathetic and working class. And I'm not worried about catching anything, as he's terribly careful and always wears a condom. Also he never kisses me on the lips.

I'd like to ask him to meet my family, but he's dead against that. Also he won't ever let me ring him. He says the man must always make the running.

I try to be patient but I'm hooked on our love life and spend my whole time feeling absolutely desperate to see him. I'm not sure why I'm writing, as it's not a problem at the moment. But will things get out of control?

A. They ARE out of control. It's a sad fact that many women have a secret longing for a man like yours - someone mad, bad and dangerous to know. But why is this Romeo alone at 45? And why does he have sex with lots of different women? Because he hasn't grown up, that's why.

And don't you think it's not only weird, but insulting, that he's never kissed you on the lips? When a man cares for a woman he wants to kiss her as lovingly and as lingeringly as possible. This man doesn't care for you at all. He's a dirty middle-aged man who can't believe his luck in being offered your lovely young body on a plate.

You've become a sex slave to him. He beckons and you come running. But you're not hooked on a love life, you're hooked on mechanical sex. The longer you stick around this bloke, the more your self-esteem will plummet. Do yourself a big favour and break this nasty habit as soon as possible.

Q. *My husband wants me to flit around the house wearing nothing but a pair of suspender tights and carrying a feather duster. Do you think I should?*

A. Only if he'll take his turn at the dusting the following week - dressed in similar garb, of course!

———————

Q. *I'm a 36 year old unmarried man. I've had many girlfriends through the years, but I'm beginning to feel a bit worried as I find I'm increasingly attracted to older women. Sometimes when I'm out, I see a girl with her mother and to my horror, it's the mother I fancy. My latest lady is 42. Do you think she's too old for me?*

A. Not at all. We women have known for years that we improve with age! As long as you and your lady like and respect each other and enjoy each other's company, where's the harm?

I have to say that no-one would bat an eyelid if YOU were the older one.

Q. For the past three or four years I've been working crazy hours trying to keep my business going during the recession.

Now I'm beginning to wonder if I've neglected my wife because she seems to have changed. Things came to a head the other night in bed. I was pretty tired, but she got me going and we ended up making love.

She asked me to imagine that I was ten years younger. This really turned her on. I asked if I should pretend to be anyone in particular. To my surprise she thought of someone immediately - an athletic looking bloke who recently moved in down the road.

My wife is quite a passionate woman anyway, but that night she was practically on fire. When she reached her climax I thought she was going to wake up the whole street!

The next morning she said she wouldn't mind acting out our fantasy and wondered whether to invite the young man down the road to join us. I want to keep her happy, as it's a real turn-on seeing her so sexually charged, but am I asking for trouble in the long run?

A. What about the SHORT run? Can't you hear danger bells ringing in your ears? You should be able to, as I can practically hear them from here! Your wife has taken a strong fancy to the hunk down the road. I can only hope that he hasn't had anything to do with her so far.

You wouldn't believe how often one marital partner innocently suggests a threesome when actually they've been having an affair with a third person for a while. I sincerely hope nothing of the sort is true in this case.

But you must act promptly. Hard though it may be, you've got to put your marriage before your business for the next few weeks. Drop everything and take your wife away somewhere warm, exotic and romantic. Pay attention to her every need and make her realise what a fool she'd be to lose a good man like you.

But on no account give in to her desire for three-way sex. This has disaster written all over it. Fantasies are fine in the mind but that's where they should stay.

Q. *My wife sometimes shouts very rude words when we make love. I'm not sure I approve of this. It's not very ladylike.*

A. Even posh ladies can go berserk in bed - and good for them! Most men adore their wives to "talk dirty" during sex. If you don't, buy some earplugs!

————

Q. *I'm an 18 year old lad and I've been going with a girl for six months. We're unemployed, but once a week we go into town and walk round the shops. Somehow she always steers me past jewellery shops. Now she's started going on about saving and complaining when I go to the pub with my mates. I like her, but her heavy-handed hints are getting me down.*

A. It's a fact of life that most young men have one thing on their mind and it ISN'T marriage! You need to think about your own future. You're not financially or emotionally ready to look after someone else. Tell this girl you've no intention of getting wed - what she then does about the relationship is up to her.

Q. Since we went back to school my life has been turned upside-down because of a new teacher. She's a real stunner with long legs, blonde hair and a great body. She's also got laughing eyes and a smile that leaves me breathless.

I'm 16 and haven't been out with a girl yet, but I know I'm totally in love with this woman. She's so much more interesting than the girls in my class.

She's married, but I know I could make her happier than her husband does. Don't tell me I'll get over it, because I won't. Just tell me what to do to make her notice me.

A. There's not much point writing to me if you don't want to hear what I've got to say!

Of course you'll get over it. Believe me, though, I do sympathise with your feelings. The first time anyone falls in love can be a devastatingly painful experience.

But let me tell you why nothing can happen between you. Firstly she would lose her job. Secondly, even if you turned out to be the stud of the century, what on earth would she talk to you about in the mornings - your maths test? Thirdly

this woman is obviously head over heels in love with her husband. Who do you think inspires the laughter in those wonderful eyes of hers?

Give yourself some time, because I'm sure that one or two girls in your class will start to seem fanciable soon.

Meanwhile be sensible and work hard in class. That'll get you noticed for the right reasons.

———

Q. *My girlfriend won't stop chewing gum while we're making love. Don't you think this is a bit off?*

A. Definitely! You should never chew gum while doing ANY form of exercise. It can be dangerous if the gum goes down the wrong way and chokes you. Also it's very rude to chew during a romantic encounter. I knew one girl who parked her gum in her boyfriend's pubic hair during oral sex. He never made love to her again!

Q. I'm a man of 68 and my lady friend is a couple of years younger. We're both trapped in loveless and sexless marriages. Some months ago we started to go for drives together in the country. We both look forward to these outings enormously.

From time to time we give each other a bit of sexual comfort - not full sex, you understand - but it does the trick.

Frankly I think I'd lose my reason if we couldn't do this. Is it terribly wrong?

A. I can't find it in my heart to tell you that it's wrong. Most of us need affection, companionship and closeness.

However, despite your ages, it's highly likely that the two of you will grow fonder and fonder of each other and fall in love. Then the occasional afternoon meeting won't be enough and you'll be consumed with a desire to spend more time together.

Have you thought how you'll feel if your secret comes out? And how you'll deal with the resulting hurt and hostility?

The other obvious question is whether you both feel too old to end these empty marriages in order to spend the rest of your lives together. Maybe you haven't dared to think of such a thing. Perhaps most of all you're afraid of what others might say?

It's time for the two of you to discuss these matters thoroughly.

You might be able to keep things just as they are, and not rock the boat. I hope you can - if that's what you want. But I'm not optimistic.

_____

Q. My new husband keeps bursting into the bathroom while I'm sitting on the toilet. I'm so embarrassed by it. Do you think I should object?

A. If it upsets you, of course you should. Togetherness is one thing, but there are certain moments when most of us would prefer to be alone!

Q. I have a big problem - the Chippendales. My girlfriend is totally obsessed by these guys. She goes to as many of their shows as she can, videos them and plasters our bedroom wall with their pictures.

I've been told that I have a great physique, but she almost ignores me nowadays. And I've gone right off sex with her because as soon as she gets worked up she yells out THEIR names - never mine. Unless this stops, I'm going to have to leave.

A. This is an outrageous blow to your pride and I'm surprised that you can raise the necessary at all, after her emasculating treatment of you.

Take action - and fast. Here's a three point plan:

* Tell your girl you're starting up a support group for all the other guys around who are suffering like you are. Then advertise locally for other blokes in the same boat. You can arrange get-togethers when the girls are at shows, or busy drooling over their pin-ups.

* Put up pin-ups of page three girls on every available bit of wall space that's left in your home. Make sure your girl sees you standing before the pictures - slavering!

* Anoint your body with baby oil and walk around the house in bathing trunks. Do this often, especially when her mum comes to tea. That ought to make your lady see sense.

But if all this fails, leave her. Your girl will soon find that videos and glossy photos are no substitute for a real live man.

———————

Q. *I'm engaged to this really handsome guy. But he never helps me around the house, never does any shopping, and so far, has never even made me a cup of tea. Do you think he'll change once we're married?*

A. Not a chance! He'll probably get worse, if that's possible. Personally I think you'd be MAD to wed.

———————

Q. *Please print this. My boyfriend always reads your column, so perhaps he will recognise himself. He's a great lad - except for one thing. His eating habits are disgusting. He chews really loudly and keeps his mouth open while he's doing it.*

It's so embarrassing for me when we go out. But he won't believe me when I tell him how revolting it looks.

A. Don't be too sure he'll recognise himself on this page. All too often folk are oblivious to their bad habits. The basic trouble here is that his eating manners are important to you while he couldn't give a damn!

Still, you could try getting someone to video him while he's chomping away, then show him the results. If that doesn't cure his slobbering habits you'll have to make a decision. Love him for what he is, or leave him.

———

Q. *I'm not sure if I have a problem or not. I've always been very keen on sex and so has my boyfriend. He's a lovely, decent, caring fella and together we've tried most things sexually, including every position you can think of.*

Recently we both decided to have our bodies pierced with jewellery before we made love. This turned out wonderfully and we were incredibly turned on.

Now we've got our nipples pierced as well as our belly buttons, noses and ears. I'm keen to have our private parts done too. But could this be harmful?

A. It takes all sorts, I suppose, but what you describe makes me feel quite sick. I've never seen the attraction in being a human pin cushion.

However, I'm prepared to accept that you have a loving and, hopefully, permanent relationship. But why do you need such zany practices to make it work? We all need variety, of course, but it sounds as if you can no longer enjoy normal cuddling, kissing and loving intercourse.

If your sex life has to get more and more extreme to be pleasurable, then I think you DO have a problem. Wacky sex could become as boring as sex in the same position once a week with the lights out. I suggest you try making love without all these extras sometimes and see how you get on.

But whatever happens PLEASE don't have your genitals pierced. The risk of infection is considerable and these tissues are very sensitive. And you don't want to damage one of your greatest assets!

Q. *When I'm in bed with my fiancée she objects to the names I use to describe her naughty bits. What could I say instead?*

A. **There are the proper Latin names, but they're awfully formal. Why don't you and your girl make up some funny words of your own?**

Q. *I met a wonderful man last year. He was charming, witty and good looking. He was also older than me. I'm 28 and he was 41.*

To my amazement he seemed to fall head over heels in love with me. He then did everything to make me fall for him. He bought me flowers and took me out for expensive meals. I'd never had so much attention or felt so loved. Bed was marvellous too. I was so turned on by him it was fantastic. I felt terrifically sexy and I was so happy I could have burst. He even started talking about marriage and though part of me felt that things were happening far too fast, I was so in love I was eager to be swept along with his ideas.

Then after a couple of months he just dropped out of my life. I've since heard that he'd done the same thing to another woman before me. I was devastated. I told him he owed me an explanation, but he just kept saying that these things happen. He made me feel as if I were hysterical and unreasonable and almost as if I'd imagined all the good times.

He did eventually say that he still cared for me, but said that marriage wouldn't work. Now all I do is cry and I've lost two stone in weight. Will he ever come back?

A. I'm afraid not and you have to accept that - tough though it is. This type of man has broken many a woman's heart, but the problem is his. He can't grow up and he can't commit permanently to a serious relationship.

He loves the chase and the excitement and maybe he even fools himself at the beginning of a new romance that this time he's ready to settle down. But he never is and his own future will be a sad and lonely one. If he gets good, professional psychological help he just MIGHT change, but this kind of guy rarely admits he's in trouble, so he never asks for help.

Try to realise that you weren't to blame. Tell yourself that if you can be loved that powerfully once, you can be again. But this time with a man who can carry things through.

Cry all you want, but look after yourself. Buy yourself little treats to eat and soak in hot scented baths - in other words think of yourself as an invalid until you start feeling brighter. Make sure that you lean on your girlfriends too - that's what they're for. One day you'll find the right partner, I'm sure, which is more than can be said for your former lover.

———————

Q. My eyesight is so bad that, when I make love to a girl, she is just a blur to me. I'd really like to wear my glasses in bed with a lady, but wonder if girls would laugh at me.

A. Some men look dreamy in specs, others frankly don't. So if you're going to do this, make sure your glasses really suit you.

I've heard that some film stars bed their women in sun glasses, so maybe tinted spectacles might be more acceptable. Contact lenses are also worth trying if your glasses make you self-conscious. But the most important thing is to find a girl who'll adore you, four-eyes and all!

Q. *My boyfriend's an amateur boxer. I hate the sport and am terrified he's going to end up brain-damaged or dead.*

A. There ARE serious accidents in boxing, though they're not common. But if your lad is keen, no amount of nagging will make him give up. If you can't cope - find another love.

Q. *I hope you can help me. I should be the happiest woman in the world, but I'm feeling very anxious.*

I've been married before and got divorced three years ago. It was a terrible marriage. Two years ago I met this wonderful, lovely man and we've been living together almost ever since.

Last night he asked me to marry him. He wants us to tie the knot next month on my fortieth birthday. I'm thrilled, but partly I'm worried that being married will change things. We're so happy. I really couldn't bear it if everything went wrong.

A. Why should it go wrong? This man isn't your ex. He's decent and caring and makes you happy. He's also a great romantic wanting to marry you on such a significant birthday!

Marriage never heals a bad or flagging relationship, but yours is neither of those things. And I bet that getting hitched will make you feel even more loved and secure than you do now. Your man has paid you a great compliment. I hope you'll go for it.

_____

Q. I've been living with a man for seven years and we both love each other very much.

But what's driving me up the wall is his quiet nature. He tells me repeatedly that he loves me, but apart from that he never talks to me about anything. I ask about his work or other things, but he cannot give me an answer.

A typical evening in our house is that he comes home, kisses me and tells me he loves me, then eats his evening meal. Unless I gossip about my day, we sit in silence for the evening. It's so bad that sometimes I dread him coming home.

A. If your man had written to me, what would he have said? Perhaps something like: "I love the woman I'm living with very much, but she does rabbit on. I tell her I love her, but this doesn't seem to be enough."

Perhaps that's unfair, but he may feel he's being interrogated. Have you enough people to talk to apart from him? Could you chat more to women friends in the day? Or could you encourage him to take up a hobby with you that you'd both enjoy, or even just organise the odd evening out which might break the silence?

At the end of the day though, you need to take on board the fact that your man clearly feels that couples who love each other should be able to enjoy companionship in silence. So you must decide whether you can continue to live with someone as quiet as him, or not.

Q. *Recently I read a letter on your page from a woman with a quiet husband. My husband is just the same. But my friend has a really gossipy husband who always has to be the centre of attention. His poor wife never gets a word in edgeways. Worse than that, she's expected to laugh at his rotten old jokes time after time. I know what sort of husband I'd sooner have and I wouldn't swap mine for the world. As for a good old natter, I can always have that with my sister or my friends.*

A. Thanks for writing. You've obviously come to terms with your quiet husband. Unfortunately my other reader hadn't. But maybe your encouragement will help her to see things in a fresh light.

———

Q. *Every Christmas we have a large family gathering at my parents'. It usually ends up with people sleeping on the floors and so on, but we all muck in and it's great. However this year turned into a nightmare.*

I woke up in the middle of Christmas night, a bit hungover, and I couldn't find my wife. I was worried, so I went round the house looking for her. I wish I hadn't, as I found her kissing and cuddling my younger brother.

They both swore it hadn't gone as far as sex, but since then my wife has been crying all the time and now she tells me that she really fancies him. She's snappy with the children and with me and is just not the girl I married.

I'm determined not to lose my wife, but even if things were different, I can't see my brother taking her on. He's only 21 and we're nearly 30. I'm sick to my guts with both of them but I want to try to save my marriage and protect our two young children.

A. Yours won't be the only household where this kind of emotional firework has exploded. It's almost inevitable where so many people are drinking too much and sleeping under the same roof.

You need to have a man-to-man talk with this young brother of yours and ask what he's playing at. But try not to knock his block off when you hear what he has to say. He may admit that he's just been trifling with your wife for a little amusement. Like you, I doubt that, at 21, he has honourable intentions such as working to provide for your wife and your kids.

Unless he and your wife are desperately in love, I think your best bet would be to try to get away for a short break with your missus. Pay her lots of attention and shower her with affection.

Once you get home continue the same treatment. With luck she'll realise that your brother was just a passing fancy. I only hope then that you can forgive AND forget.

———

Q. I'm 21 and have been going out with my girlfriend for just over a year. I like her a lot. In fact I've never felt this way about a girl before. I look forward to being with her, and when we meet up I feel comfortable and good.

However, she's taken our relationship more seriously than me right from the start. But now, because I want to keep her happy and also don't want to lose her, I've proposed.

She's thrilled - she accepted right away. Her parents, who are very nice, are pleased for us too. But my mum and dad think I'm too young and hope that we'll wait several years before marrying.

My parents' attitude has made me think again. Although my girlfriend is special, I'm frightened by the thought of trying to be faithful to her for the rest of my life. Also I know that I still fancy other girls. Is this normal and will I get over it? Or do you think I should break off our engagement? If so, how can I do it without upsetting her?

A. Like lots of 21 year old girls, your lady's keen to settle down. She's probably got the wedding planned in her mind already and may even have started to think about names for your future children!

But you're different. I suspect you proposed in the heat of the moment and now you feel trapped. This is natural in a young male, and plenty of blokes reading this page will sympathise.

It would be folly to even THINK about marrying until you're older and have lived a bit more. So you must level with your girlfriend. But please do it gently. She's doubtless excited to be engaged, so try to help her to realise that your reluctance isn't her fault. That should help her self-respect if nothing else.

Tell her how much you value her, but say that you've realised you're not as mature as her and that you're not ready to make commitments. You may lose her through your honesty, but that would surely be better than marrying too young. If she's reasonable she may continue to see you. And if that happens it would be a nice gesture to buy her a ring - not an engagement one - just something to assure her of your fond friendship.

_____

Q. I admit that years ago I was a bit of a lad. When my wife was busy with our two young kids, I had odd affairs with other women, though none of them meant much. But my wife found out about some of them and was upset, so I decided to mend my ways. I haven't had another woman now for five years and I thought we had quite a happy marriage.

Recently, the second of our kids left home. Since then my wife's done nothing but cry, and last night she said she wants a divorce. I can't talk any sense into her. Why is she behaving like this?

A. The children gave your wife a reason for living. And, I daresay, they were her only source of company when you were playing fast and loose with other women.

Maybe she saved her sanity all those years ago by promising herself a fresh life when the kids grew up. Or maybe she's just looked round her "empty nest" and decided she can't face living with you - alone. You could try to talk to her, or suggest the two of you visit Relate. You could even arrange a trip away, but my guess is that her mind is made up.

Q. *My wife and I are both in our mid-thirties. We've got two little girls of 10 and 8. Last year we went through a bad patch and I had an affair with a woman at work. I told my wife about it and she went crazy. Next thing I knew SHE was having an affair with my best friend. His wife found out and all hell broke loose.*

Anyway we decided that, for the sake of our kids, we'd try to save our marriage. So we've been having a romantic night out together once a week and we're also trying to be more considerate towards each other.

But now my wife wants another baby. I think it's too soon after all the trouble. Who's right?

A. It's not a question of right and wrong. You've both been marvellously sensible in working out ways in which you can save your marriage. And I'm sure you'll do it.

Your wife's response to this extra love and emotion has been to get broody, while you're anxious that such a move might create more stress. Both views are understandable, but I'd advise caution for a while. Why not agree that you'll discuss the issue again in a year's time, if all goes well.

———————

Q. *My husband drives trucks here and on the continent. He works hard and earns good money. But I want him to give up the job, as I'm fed up coping with two bairns on my own - he's away a large part of every month. He says it would kill him to be out of work and he doesn't think he'd get a job if he gave up this one - where we live loads of men are unemployed. He also says that I knew what his job was when I married him.*

I'm trying to see his point of view, but it's hard, and often, even when he DOES come home, all I do is nag him.

A. I'm sure it's hell on wheels coping with two little ones on your own. But I beg you to consider what life would be like if your husband were at home under your feet - miserable, with no money or a job. That would put a far greater strain on your marriage and might kill your husband's spirit for good. I bet there are lots of wives like you. Why don't you start a club so that you can all support each other and baby-sit for each other from time to time. Then, when your husband comes home, you'll be less stressed and more able to welcome him with love and open arms.

———

Q. I got married just over a year ago. My wife is a nice person who's always backed me one hundred per cent. We always got on well enough and I think a lot of her. She has a lot of love to give, but I've never truly felt she was right for me.

A couple of months after our marriage I met someone who immediately clicked with me. She's the sort of girl I've been looking for all my life. Though we tried to fight it, we started having an affair. We love each other desperately.

I told my wife and she took an overdose. Later she admitted that she only did it to get back at me. I stopped seeing the other girl for a while, but we were both so unhappy, we're now having an affair again.

Unfortunately my wife has recently had a breakdown and spent time in hospital. And now we seem very bitter towards each other. I can't bear to cause her pain, she really doesn't deserve it. But I sometimes believe that, if I stay with her, it'll be worse in the long run as my heart will always be with the other girl. I've never hurt anyone in my life. Please help.

A. I wish you'd never married - I expect you do too. It sounds as if you tied the knot simply because someone was offering affection and support. Or maybe you thought it was time to get wed - perhaps lots of your mates had got married. Whatever your reasons, you doubtless thought that the sort of love that stops you in your tracks was not for you. Then - WHAM! - a lady came along who proved that breathless romance DOESN'T just happen in films or books and you were knocked sideways.

But to be fair to your marriage vows, you ought to give up your lover and have no contact at all with her for three months. This MIGHT work and you may be able to rebuild your marriage.

But if, as I suspect, you and your wife have lost whatever it was that once made your relationship viable, you should both accept it and call it a day now, while the two of you are still young and childless.

If this happens, you'll then be free to pursue the other relationship. I can only hope that you'll put all your energy into it and make it for keeps.

———

Q. *I'm 18 and find myself very attracted to a girl who has a bit of a reputation in our town. She's had quite a few blokes, if you know what I mean.*

Anyway, I really like her. But do you think I'm interested because I suspect she knows more about sex than other girls, or because I genuinely like her personality?

A. A bit of both, I should think. The chances are that this girl hasn't had as many men as her reputation suggests. But whatever her tally, no-one would be questioning it if she were male! These double standards still exist, even in the nineties.

Quite often girls like this one are really unhappy. They're searching for something that none of their one-night stands ever provides - qualities like care and decency and companionship and love.

Maybe you could be different and treat her like a human being. But you won't forget to wear a condom will you?

———————

Q. *For three months I've been seeing the sexiest woman I've ever known.*

She's older than me - about 35 - and her husband left her for a younger girl last year.

I think she's still in love with her old man - even though she calls him vile names - because sometimes when we make love she bursts into tears.

Sex is fantastic, but I think she's using me as a stud and at the end of every session she turns nasty and tells me to go. Do we have a future?

A. Not outside of the bedroom, I'm afraid. I'm sure this woman is still bitter and hurt about her husband leaving her. Half of her hates him, but the other half still loves him madly.

The strange thing is that women often feel terrifically sexy when they're in this kind of trouble.

Clearly she needs good sex and you provide it, but deep down she knows that you're the wrong man. So when sex is over she feels guilty and wants to punish you both. That's why she gets you to leave as soon as possible.

If you don't mind being used for your equipment alone, then stick around. But don't kid yourself that this is a proper relationship.

Q. My *wife says that she can't stand my attitude to personal hygiene any longer. She says I don't wash my hair or my body nearly often enough. She'd also like me to shave more and pay more attention to my teeth.*

Now she says if I won't smarten up, there'll be no more sex. Do you think she's serious?

A. I doubt if she's ever been more serious in her life. Poor woman - God knows what it must be like to live with you.

It's time for you to turn over a new leaf. If you won't, I fear you'll end up alone.

————————

Q. *I'm shortly to marry a lovely boy who happens to be an epileptic. He hasn't had any fits now for several years, but he still has to take medicine every day.*

I feel I ought to know more about his condition. I want to know whether it could affect our children, and also how I would cope if it got worse.

A. Your boyfriend's epilepsy is obviously well under control and with a loving wife beside him he should do even better.

But you're sensible to want to know more. The National Society for Epilepsy has a family membership scheme. For details call 0494-873991.

Q. *My girlfriend is 16, but she says she's still too young to go all the way. Is she right?*

A. No-one should have sex until they really want to. So respect that and DON'T bully her.

Q. *I'm 26 and I married very young at 16. I have six children and a husband who adores me. But he won't let me do ANYTHING on my own. I can't even speak to my brother on the phone when my husband is at home.*

If I say I want to go out with the girls, he kicks up such a fuss that I end up not going.

He's a good man and he works hard for the kids and me, but if I don't get an identity of my own soon, I'm going to go mad.

Don't write to me privately because he will flip and I can't stand any more hassle.

A. You're not a pet rabbit waiting for the master to open your hutch occasionally and give you a stroke. You're a grown woman and your husband's behaviour is INTOLERABLE.

Yet I can see that he loves you desperately. He would go to pieces if he lost you. But that's just what WILL happen, unless he mends his ways.

First you must decide how much time you'd like to yourself each week. Then decide what you'll do with it. Perhaps you want to go out with friends, or maybe you'd like to go on a course to learn something new. Once you know what you want to do, then somebody - possibly you - has to tell your husband. If you can't tell him to his face, then write him a letter. or get someone to talk to him for you - a friend or a relative.

He has to understand three things:-

* You love him
* You need some time to yourself
* If you don't get it, you'll leave

Stick to your guns and also try to persuade him to go with you for some counselling at Relate.

You say yourself he's a good man, so hang on in there, if you can.

———————————

Q. *I was looking forward to Christmas Eve as I thought my boyfriend might propose. My best friend was getting engaged at Christmas and I thought it would be great if I did too.*

We went out to the pub and had quite a nice time with some of my boyfriend's mates. Then he walked me home and said he wouldn't be able to see me for a few days. I was a bit upset about that and he never said anything about getting engaged. So I told him I loved him - I'd never done that before. But he didn't say it back - just sort of grunted. Now I feel stupid.

A. Don't worry, love. I made the same mistake with my first boyfriend. When I plucked up courage to say that I loved him, he just said "I know!" - I never did that again!

Like you, I'd thought all I wanted in life was to get married.

But, fortunately, soon afterwards I realised that I didn't even like my boyfriend all that much. Then I began to see that life could be much more interesting if I stayed single for a good few years to come. Maybe you should do the same?

———

Q. I go to a fitness centre to work out. I work shifts, so I'm often there during the day when a lot of middle-aged women attend the place. One of these women - who's obviously well off and quite attractive for her age - seems to have taken to me in a big way. She's always pointing me out to her friends and sometimes makes an excuse to touch my body while I'm training.

But the other day things went further. I was leaving the swimming pool while she was in it and she managed to *pull down my trunks as I walked up the steps. She was laughing and said she'd give me "ten out of ten."*

Then last week she offered me cash to pose in the nude - she says she's an amateur painter. I've told my girlfriend about this, but she's not worried and she says if there's money in it, I should do it.

I can't help but be flattered by this woman's attention and I suppose it could all be harmless fun, but I'm worried in case she's working round to having sex with me. I don't fancy her, I'm afraid, so I'm not sure what to do next.

A. I'm sure your original plan at this fitness centre was to tone your muscles, and it sounds as if you're in great shape. But your middle-aged lady obviously has designs on one specific part of your body and wants you to exercise it in her private company!

Frankly, I think your girlfriend's MAD not to mind. I'd be baying for this woman's blood if you were my man. I must also say that if you were a woman writing about this kind of sexual harassment by a man, I'd be furious, on your behalf, at your partner's lack of concern. But on top of that, I'd be advising you to take legal action.

However, you're a big boy and able to take care of yourself, I'm sure. But I beg you to think twice before you get more involved, as I believe things could get nasty.

If you were attracted to this woman, I'd suggest that you pose for fun, NOT money and take it from there - so long as you took along a stack of condoms! But you DON'T want to have sex with her, so why cheapen yourself before her? I should call a halt to her fun and games now. You're obviously not happy about it, otherwise you wouldn't have written to me, would you?

———

Q. *Last spring I was working away from home when I had a few dates with a girl. We got on quite well and made love a few times, but I always wore a condom.*

After I'd gone home she contacted me to say she was pregnant. I didn't want any fuss so I agreed to pay her some money every week to support the child.

But now I keep reading all about the Child Support Agency, I'm worried that I might have to pay a lot more.

*And the thing is that I'm not sure that the baby is mine.
I've seen it a couple of times and have no feelings for it.
And I can't help wondering if this girl was seeing other
blokes - blokes who weren't wearing condoms. How can
I find out for sure if the child is mine?*

A. The best way is through DNA testing, though
this is likely to cost you about £450 in total, as the
child and its mother will have to be tested as well as
you. If you ARE the dad, there'll be no escaping
the fact, if that's what the test shows. But since
there does seem to be some doubt about this child,
I think you should send for a DNA enquiry pack
from University Diagnostics Limited. Call:- 071-
401-9898.

---

*Q. I'm a nurse and throughout my marriage I've worked
in the private sector as we needed the money. I've paid for
most things at home including our occasional holidays.
My husband has never stuck at any job for long. When
we had our two children he volunteered to stay at home to
look after them - which he did until they went to
playschool. But he wasn't very good with them - he probably just preferred being at home to working.*

He's a difficult man and has no real friends. Even his mother and other relatives only tolerate him in small doses. I think I fell for him because he was so hopeless and needed looking after - and that's what I'm good at.

But after eighteen years of it, I'm worn out. I feel I give and do everything and get nothing in return. Also I'm sick to death of my husband's surly and miserable manner.

Our children are almost grown up and they keep out of their father's way as much as possible. I'd like us to separate, but worry what will happen to him if I do.

A. Men like your husband always survive when their poor, exhausted, guilt-ridden wives finally give them the elbow. I bet he'll get his feet under another woman's table in no time.

You've given your all to this marriage and have nothing left to give. Maybe if your man had been charming, a wonderful father and a tireless lover, you'd have happily continued organising and paying for everything. But it sounds as if he contributed nothing to your marriage, except to give you someone to look after when you needed it.

He may be depressed, in which case he should see his doctor, but this shouldn't stop you from carving out a new life for yourself.

You're easily young enough to meet someone else, but, even if you never do, my guess is that you'll enjoy each day far more without the millstone of your lazy, unproductive husband hanging round your neck.

However, before you do anything, please speak to the Citizens' Advice Bureau about your legal rights. You might find your husband will expect you to continue to keep him, as you've been the bread-winner throughout the marriage.

Q. *Since my divorce I've lived alone. It hasn't been easy, but I've enjoyed great companionship from my two cats.*

For the past six months I've had a relationship with a nice man who's also divorced. We get on well in and out of bed and last week he proposed.

The only problem is that he hates cats. He's made no effort to get to know mine and if I marry him, he'll expect me to go and live with him and my cats would not be welcome. What should I do?

A. I can't tell you, I'm afraid. And I don't envy you your decision.

At the end of the day I can't help but feel that a real, living, breathing man is more important than two cats. But I do know from experience how lonely life is after divorce and how very comforting a pet can be.

Maybe you can compromise and find your cats a new home where you'll be welcome to visit? But you MAY decide that, as an animal lover, you can't be truly happy with a man who isn't.

———

Q. I'm 19 and I've been going out with my girlfriend for two years. For a few months now I've been feeling that I just don't like her as much as I once did. There's nothing wrong with her exactly, I've just gone off her, I suppose.

The trouble is that I'm falling for her best friend. But the last thing I want to do is to hurt my girlfriend. Somehow I must break out, as I feel I'm in a rut, but how can I do it without causing pain?

A. You can't. It's not your fault that you've come to the end of this relationship. These things happen. And don't make the mistake of prolonging the romance just because you feel sorry for your girl. Some men even marry in such circumstances, so as not to upset the "little woman." But it's always a bad mistake and no basis for matrimony. The kindest thing would be to finish with your long-term lover, then wait some weeks before asking her friend out. That way your girl should be able to retain some dignity.

———————

Q. *My wife and I have been married for fourteen years. We have two lovely children. But recently she's been impossible. She hasn't a good word to say for anyone and she's in a bad mood all the time. As for sex, she's always making excuses. I suggested she see our doctor, but she wouldn't. Please can you help. I don't think I can put up with this much longer.*

A. I'm sorry about this - your life sounds like a nightmare. But people don't change suddenly for no reason. It might be that your wife is worried about money, or about getting older, or about her job or her family. I'm afraid it's also possible that she's fallen for someone else, although I hope that's not the case.

I suggest you take her to a quiet pub one evening, sit her down with a large brandy and gently persuade her to tell you what's going on. There must be something, and whatever it is, I'm sure you'll both be able to start dealing with it once it's out in the open. Good luck.

———

Q. My job keeps me away from home a couple of nights a week. Recently I asked my wife if she missed me sexually while I'm away.

She said she could always "see to herself if need be." Does this mean what I think it does? I'm not sure it's very nice behaviour for a married lady?

A. All your wife means is that she masturbates. Join the modern world! Recent sex surveys have shown that many women masturbate.

Just be grateful that your wife sticks to DIY and doesn't move in a toy-boy when you're out of town.

Male Sex Problems

These account for the lion's share of my postbag from men. From the earliest age, a boy is fascinated by sex. He's interested in how his body works and is desperate to grow up with all his bits the right size and in the right places.

Most men have anxieties, but they usually don't discuss them together. A man will happily tell his cronies that he "got his leg over" so and so last night. But he'll never tell his mates if things went badly, let alone ask if anyone else has had the same trouble.

That's why men write to people like me. And, thank goodness, quite often I'm able to reassure them or point them in the direction of professional medical help that will sort them out.

I've included masturbation in this section - not that I think it's a problem - because I don't. It's a natural and safe way to enjoy some sexual activity. But even nowadays people get very hot under the collar about it. So I hope that this section of the book will put a few people's minds at rest.

Q. *I'm a guy of 24. A few years ago I used to be able to "do it" five times a night. But now I can only manage it twice!*

Surely I shouldn't be going off the boil at my age?

A. Relax - you're not over the hill yet!

Most young men start off with the ability to have lots of orgasms in an evening, but as you get older your score will drop.

Never mind. As you mature, you'll get lots more control which should make you a better lover and help you to have deeply satisfying climaxes. Quality is the keyword, NOT quantity!

Q. *I'm a lad of 16. Last month I lost my virginity to a woman of 40. It was great, but was it illegal?*

A. No - as long as it was after your sixteenth birthday. I'm pleased you enjoyed this, but please don't repeat it. Older women who like to seduce teenagers can be a bit dodgy.

Q. *I hope you can help me. At a friend's party a couple of weeks ago, I met a very sexy lady who was much older than me.*

We ended up having intercourse. Luckily I wore a condom. But can you get a venereal disease or even AIDS through caressing someone's private parts?

You see, because of my work, my fingers are quite cracked and I have odd cuts on them. Could a disease attack me through my hands? I've since heard that this woman will go with anybody, so I'm very worried.

A. It's most unlikely that you've caught anything through the cuts on your fingers. However, I'm sorry to say that it is just POSSIBLE.

If you want to find out for sure, ring your nearest big hospital and ask for the Genito-Urinary Medicine Clinic. They'll invite you to come along for a chat, and maybe some tests too.

Q. *You told a couple that getting a vibrator would help their marriage. I can't say that I agree. I was perfectly happily married for years and my sex life was fine, even though my wife never reached orgasm.*

But after we got a vibrator, my wife became addicted to it. She then lost interest in me and now we're divorced.

A. So you think your sex life was fine, do you? Fine for you, no doubt, but obviously an absolute misery for your poor, frustrated wife. No wonder she got hooked on the vibrator - she was making up for a lot of lost time and disappointment.

It sounds to me as if your selfishness ended your life together -NOT the vibrator.

Q. *I'm 18 and my girlfriend is 15. Is it OK to make love?*

A. Well, intercourse is not legal until she's 16. So, until then, try to curtail your activities to love play.

Q. My sex life with my girlfriend is great. But I was stunned the other day when she said how pleased she was that I am so well endowed. She claimed that small fellas don't get her going nearly so well.

Don't the experts say that size isn't important.

A. Men can satisfy women in a variety of ways, many of which have nothing to do with the man's penis. So from that point of view, size is totally unimportant.

But many women do like a bit of bulk. And why not? After all it's OK for men to say they prefer girls with big boobs or long legs.

Anyway, your girl obviously thinks you measure up just fine. So what are you worried about?

———

Q. I am a man of 70 and last year I lost my wife through cancer. I was still deeply in love with her and almost right up to the end we had a happy and fulfilling sexual relationship. It's this part of our life together that I miss most now. I can't tell anyone else that, but I feel I can tell you.

What I do now is to buy a girlie magazine when I go into town once a week for my shopping. I wouldn't like anyone to know this, but I feel I need the help I get from this in order to get an erection. Masturbation on its own is quite difficult for me.

Do you think I'm a disgusting old man?

A. Certainly not. I think what you are doing is wise and sensible. Masturbation is the safest form of sex that there is. Some men in your position would choose to go to prostitutes instead. But masturbation is cheaper and there's no attendant health hazard. As to the girlie pictures, if this is what you need to get you going - relax and enjoy it!

Q. I'm a divorced man of 41. Since my divorce my sex life seems to have gone haywire. I'm not always confident I can get a full erection. But, worse than that, I climax far too quickly - in fact, sometimes I don't even achieve penetration. Now, after a few brief romances, I've found a really wonderful woman. She's been very kind and understanding about my problems, but I don't want to lose her because I can't satisfy her.

A. Relax! Divorce is one of the most stressful episodes in anyone's life. So it's hardly surprising that all your bits can't behave as if nothing has happened.

Your new relationship sounds very promising, but don't rush it. While some women enjoy a robust sex session, many of them would sooner be satisfied in other ways. So take the pressure off yourself by caressing and stroking your lady with your fingers and tongue and concentrating on her pleasure.

But if, after a while, your own performance is still troubling you, make an appointment at your local Family Planning Clinic. A doctor there should be able to improve things dramatically.

Q. I'm a 33 year old man who's desperate for a sex change. I've felt this way since I was 12. Loads of people have tried to talk me out of it, but they don't understand. You see, deep down inside I FEEL like a woman. Is there a doctor who would help me?

A. You're embarking on a long and demanding process. You'll need hormone treatment and then you'll have to live as a woman for two years before a surgeon will consider you for surgery. Your first move should be to contact the Gender Dysphoria Trust International helpline on: 0323-641100. They'll give you the information and support that you need.

———

Q. *My mate reckons I'm gay because I haven't gone all the way with my girlfriend. But I really like her and don't want to try anything too soon in case I lose her.*

A. Tell your mate he could learn some lessons in romance from you!

———

Q. *I'm a very virile fellow who needs sex regularly. But every time I reach out for my wife she turns away from me. This is driving me mad. I don't feel I can go on without the release of good sex. Surely she shouldn't refuse me my basic rights? Please help me before I go completely round the bend.*

A. I'm sure that this no-sex situation is making you pretty ratty, but I can't help wondering what your wife's version of this state of affairs might be.

I find it quite disturbing that you never say in your letter that you love her. What you DO say is that you're virile and need sex. How romantic can you get? Then you talk about "basic rights" as if all women should drop everything - literally - if their lord and master fancies a bonk. This is a very old-fashioned view of marriage.

Do you talk together? Do you share hobbies? Do you bring her presents, or tell her she looks nice? Have a think about it. The chances are that she's refusing sex because something in your relationship has gone badly wrong. I hope you're prepared to work to put it right.

Q. We've been married for a year and are very happy, except for one thing. My wife reaches orgasm quite easily, but it takes me ages. In fact sometimes I don't get there at all. This leaves her tired and sore and me fed up and frustrated. What can I do?

A. This is rotten for you, but please try to understand that many men have this problem. Its posh name is "Ejaculatory Incompetence."

Some men who suffer from it are actually very popular with the ladies as they can keep going far, far longer than the average bloke.

For a woman who needs a lot of build-up to her climax, this can be marvellous. The problem comes in a long-term relationship like yours where the wife climaxes easily, or when a couple want children.

So make an appointment at your local Family Planning Clinic. They'll teach you to overcome this problem without any embarrassment. It'll probably take several sessions, and your wife will need to go with you. But results are generally excellent.

Q. Since my wife left me and we divorced three years ago, I find that I'm only attracted by big women. Slim model girls do absolutely nothing for me. In fact they turn me right off. You'll probably tell me that my sexual tastes are horrible and disgusting, but I need a LARGE woman and there don't seem to be many about.

A. You're not horrible or disgusting. What about the blokes who only like women with long legs? And what about girls who only fancy men with small bottoms? They're not all perverts, you know. Many men like large ladies. They feel secure and cherished and mothered by women with fuller figures. And when you think that at least a third of women in this country are technically overweight, it's not realistic to say that you don't meet any.

Your real problem is that your confidence has taken a severe knock. It's time to start enjoying your single life. When you feel happier with yourself, the woman of your dreams - large or small - will probably walk into your life.

Q. I am a soldier serving in Northern Ireland. The worst thing about it is not having sex with my girlfriend. Obviously I masturbate a great deal while I'm away. I'm not proud of this, but if I didn't do it, I reckon I'd go mad. Last time I was home I made love to my girl as soon as I could. To my embarrassment, I came almost immediately. I've never had a problem like this before. Do you think it's because I've been doing a lot of masturbating?

A. No, I don't. I think you feel sex-starved in Northern Ireland - and who wouldn't. You obviously see masturbation as a very second-rate activity compared with intercourse, so when you see your lady you're desperate to have her.

If you could only discuss this problem with some of your mates you'd probably find that many of them have had the same difficulty. So next time you're home, tell your girl you're mad for her and just laugh if you come a bit too quickly. You can always have sex again soon after - and again and again!

Q. I think I may be a sex addict. Things weren't too bad when my wife and I were first married, but they went wrong when our children were small. Then I got heavily involved in sex chat lines which cost me a fortune. But at least they were harmless apart from that. Now I can't keep away from clubs where all sorts of odd people go. I know I'm in danger, but can't seem to stop myself.

A. There's been a lot in the papers about sex addiction in the last few months. Some experts reckon it's a real syndrome, others claim it's just an excuse for outrageous and immature behaviour. You could ask your doctor if he or she knows of any therapy you could get on the NHS, but I suspect that there won't be any.

Your local Citizens' Advice Bureau should have details of private counselling in your area and likely charges. It's possible that someone nearby is specialising in your problem.

The other suggestion I have is Alcoholics Anonymous. Whether or not you drink heavily, it's likely that your need for sex is much like an alcoholic's need for drink and you may find help there. Others have tried and succeeded, so I hope you'll give it a go.

————

Q. *I'm not very successful with women and I wonder if it's because they think my penis is too small. Do you know of any exercises that can make it bigger?*

A. No. I've sometimes heard of men who've tried hanging weights on their pride and joy, but that sounds a barmy idea to me. You could easily get damaged and ruin yourself for good and all.

If you're not doing too well with the ladies, I doubt very much if it has anything to do with your equipment. Much more likely that you don't make them laugh, or that you don't ask them about themselves, or listen to what they have to say.

Most women are looking for a bit of reassurance and they need to feel a man is really interested in THEM and not just desperate to get their knickers down. So why not concentrate on getting to know women properly and forget about the size of your manhood, which is probably absolutely fine.

———

Q. I'm a 27 year old, single man. I haven't had sex with a woman for nearly three years. It's not that I'm off women - quite the reverse - or that I don't get any offers. It's just that I can't seem to get an erection once I get close to a girl. I have plenty of erections on my own, so do you think I'm too anxious when I get near a woman?

A. Yes, I do. There's absolutely nothing physically wrong with you. So I imagine you just have a bit of a bee in your bonnet about performing with a woman, or satisfying her. Why not broaden your education by learning a few techniques from a good sex video like *The Lovers' Guide*. The more you know, the more confident you'll feel.

Also, when you meet a woman, try to get to know her properly. Talk to her and listen to what she has to say. If you get wrapped up in a woman's personality you'll be less anxious about sex. But if things don't improve, ring your local Family Planning Clinic and ask them to recommend a psycho-sexual counsellor.

———

Q. How often is it safe to make love? I'd like to do it twice a day, every day. My girlfriend thinks that it will cause us some damage. We're both 20. Is she right?

A. Not exactly. At your age I can see no reason why lovemaking twice daily should damage you physically, but it might end your relationship. Your girlfriend clearly thinks your demands are a bit excessive. Maybe you're not very considerate about her satisfaction. Or perhaps you're too rough. Sex isn't an Olympic event - yet. And girls like romance and cuddling as well as a pumping performance!

Next time you make love, stop wondering how soon you might do it again, and concentrate instead on making that encounter a really special, delicious experience for your girlfriend. I'm sure that she'll be grateful - and show it!

———————

Q. *My problem is my wife's sister. She's only 14, but it's obvious that she's a right sex kitten.*

Since my wife and I had our two children, we've had our ups and downs. When we first married she was dead keen on sex. Then after the kids she didn't seem interested.

This really hurt me, so I had an affair with a woman at work. Fortunately I quickly saw that I might lose my wife and family through this stupidity, so I ended it. Then my wife and I started really working at our marriage and things are much better now.

I like to take her out one evening a week and that's where her sister comes in. She baby-sits. But I have to run her back home afterwards because it's too late for her to get a bus.

In the meantime find your own female company. I bet lots of other girls would like to go out with you. And it shouldn't be too long before someone nice offers to help you lose your virginity.

———

Q. My girlfriend is usually quiet and a bit prim and proper. But now I've seen another side to her.

A few weeks ago she came round to my house and told me she had a pleasant surprise for me. It was a pair of black leather trousers. She insisted I put them on immediately, which I did. She then started calling me her leather-clad stud and using explicit language that I've never heard her say before.

At first I found this a turn-on and we made the most exciting love ever. But since then she's refused to have ordinary sex and will only do it if I'm in the trousers.

I'm now beginning to feel very awkward and uncomfortable about it. I've tried talking to her, but all she'll say is that sex is better for her like that and if I won't give in to her, she'll find someone who will. I don't want to lose her, so what can I do?

A. Lots of people relish something a bit different sexually once in a while. I know one woman who goes wild when her husband wears his thigh-high fishing waders! But it's like eating cream cakes - lovely occasionally, but nauseating and also harmful if you do it all the time. Obviously your girlfriend has some problem in communicating normally - you describe her as prim and proper. Maybe the only way she can get aroused and throw caution to the winds is by using leather. But if you never make love normally, I think you'll resent it and may even find your performance suffers. Also you'll probably die of boredom!

Try asking her if she'd like to try anything else. If this doesn't work tell her you'll only wear the trousers once a week - that seems a fair compromise. But if she can't see sense, you must ask yourself whether you REALLY want to be in this relationship - leather and all - or whether you'd prefer someone with more conventional tastes.

Counselling at Relate could help, but my guess is that your girl sees nothing odd in her own behaviour, so may well refuse to go.

Male and Female Sex Problems

Sometimes it's hard to determine whether the problem is a male or a female one. These three letters will show you what I mean:

———

Q. *I've just got married and I love it all. I only have one slight reservation and that is that my husband seems to be obsessed by his penis. He spends ages soaping it in the bath. And he's always asking me if I like it and keeps wanting me to touch it. Are all men like this?*

A. Mostly! Men begin a love affair with their manhood the day they're born. This is difficult for women to understand, since we tend to think our private parts are ugly.

Your man is probably desperate to make an impression on you and is anxious for reassurance.

Tell him he looks marvellous and that the sight of him turns you on. He'll love you for it.

Sensible wives regard hubby's favourite bit as a shared hobby. Much like going with him to the football - but more agreeable!

———

Q. *My husband is wonderful and totally outrageous in bed - but he's very noisy.*

When we make love he shouts and yells for joy at the top of his voice. This is fine by me at home where we have thick walls. In fact it's a big turn-on. But last week he did it when we stayed with my mother and I didn't know where to put myself at the breakfast table next morning.

A. I wouldn't have been brave enough to go down to breakfast myself - so well done you!

Isn't it marvellous that you have such a great time together. Mind you, I DO see your problem. Have you ever been thrown out of a hotel?

All I can suggest is that, when you're away on a short trip, you try satisfying your husband with your hands or your mouth. He's unlikely to be so loud climaxing in either of these ways. I think it's all that thrusting during intercourse that does it. But if this doesn't work, then brazen it out. If anyone gives you a funny look in the morning, just put it down to jealousy.

———

Q. Could you tell me how much foreplay a woman should want. My first wife wasn't really bothered, but the girlfriend I have now likes a lot of warming up. I sometimes can't quite believe it can take that long, though she certainly enjoys sex when we get on to it.

A. Every woman is different. To make life even MORE difficult the same woman can act very differently on different days! The important thing is that your lady is properly ready for full sex when you get there. It sounds as if she's enjoying herself, so you must be doing OK.

But I sense a certain impatience and I hope it won't get out of hand. Men are often very considerate at the beginning of a relationship, but get lazy later. Don't let that happen to you.

Remember that, for many women, love play is just as good if not better than intercourse. And women love to kiss - something that men often forget. I suggest you buy yourself a good sex education book and learn how to spot the signs of when a woman is really getting aroused.

Female Sex Problems

Q. Something happened last week that changed my life. I feel so different that I keep looking in the mirror to see if I've altered. It started when my husband brought home a naughty video. At first I was a bit annoyed. I felt as if he was telling me that our sex life wasn't good enough.

Anyway, he persuaded me to watch it and I was shocked to find that I was completely carried away. I wasn't myself at all. Normally I'm not very passionate - in fact I've never had a climax with my husband, although I've managed it on my own. But that night everything was so wonderful and easy. I couldn't get enough - I was like an animal on heat. I was almost frightened at being so turned on and I was very noisy, which is totally unlike me.

We watched the video twice, making love all the while until we were both exhausted. I feel a little ashamed that I let myself go in this way, but my husband is thrilled. However, I'm worried that it'll only work like that with a video. Am I some sort of a pervert?

A. Absolutely not - all that's happened is that you've had some overdue orgasms, so stop worrying. You've discovered the key to your sexier self, and you have your husband to thank for this, so I hope you'll find a suitable way to thank him! But that's just the beginning.

What you must do is to build a fulfilling sex life on the foundation that you laid the other day. Make love as often as you can. Try new things and allow hidden feelings to surface. Show your man what turns you on. Don't be shy. This could take years off both of you!

And you needn't be anxious that you won't be able to "do it" without a video. I'm sure you'll use videos again, but they'll just become ONE of the ways you can get aroused. Remember variety is the spice of love.

So take it in turns to please each other and decide what's on the sex menu of the day. Try a romantic session in a secluded spot out of doors - when the weather's nice. Or take a bath together and massage each other's bodies - this could lead to explosive sex! The world of love is yours - enjoy it.

Q. *My boyfriend just refuses to wear a condom. What can I do?*

A. Simple! Tell him: "No condom, no sex." That should change his mind.

———————

Q. *My husband wants me to wear edible knickers which he has bought in a sex shop. The idea is that he wants to nibble them off me, and then have oral sex. Isn't this a bit peculiar?*

A. Well, I have heard that undies like these have a really yukky taste. Still - perhaps your old man has a very sweet tooth! If you feel turned on and happy with what he proposes to do, then throw caution to the winds and just enjoy it. But if you feel that this kind of love play isn't for you, then tell him to forget it.

———————

Q. *My girlfriend and I think the world of each other, but our love-making is constantly interrupted by her insisting that I'm too big.*

I've tried to get an answer about this problem from reading various books on sex and watching The Lovers' Guide video, but I'm still a bit in the dark. I do everything I can to make sure she's really ready for intercourse. And she says she feels turned on by me, but I still cause her pain.

What can I do?

A. I'm sure you're not too big. Don't forget that the insides of a woman are very elastic, otherwise she couldn't have babies. So your girlfriend can't be too small for you.

It's much more likely that she has some deep-seated fear about being penetrated and has convinced herself that it's bound to hurt.

Take her to a Family Planning Clinic where a doctor will demonstrate to her how expandable a woman's equipment really is. The doctor will also teach her to relax. This should put things right between you.

Q. I'm 21 and totally confused about my sexuality. As a teenager I loathed looking female and didn't want to develop breasts - I hated them.

I've had sex with men, but I hated that too. Then recently at a social gathering, a group of women arrived together. When they looked at me I felt great. One of them asked if I was gay and I said that I was. But am I?

A. It's possible. But it may not be as simple as that. Gay women don't often hate breasts - their own, or other women's - because they're so much a part of being female.

However it's clear that you find the prospect of contact with other women more appealing than your dealings with men.

I suggest that you call the Gay and Lesbian Switchboard for a chat. Their 24 hour number is: 071-837-7324. (You may have to persist to get through). They'll point you in the direction of the help you need and also tell you about activities and clubs in your own area.

Q. *My breasts get quite tender before my period. I cope with this quite well except when it comes to making love. My boyfriend is definitely a breast man, but on those days his attentions leave me very sore. What can I do?*

A. A lot of women swear by Primrose Oil capsules to cut down on premenstrual breast tenderness. Vitamin B6 is thought to help too.

As for your boyfriend, explain to him, gently, that you can't enjoy breast play at such times. If he ignores you, or just forgets to keep away from them, you might decide to write him a message in lipstick across your boobs - something like "OFF LIMITS" should do the trick!

Q. *My husband is always thinking up new ways to spice up our sex life. Now he wants to introduce whipped cream into our love play. Is there any harm in this?*

A. Not unless you're on a low fat diet!

Q. Last week I got engaged, and for the first time my fiancé and I had full sex. It was exciting, but I was nervous. I was also worried that I was too dry inside. Can you help?

A. This often happens when couples aren't very experienced. You should make sure that you and your lad go in for plenty of love play - stroking and kissing and fondling - before he attempts to enter you. That should get your natural juices flowing freely. But if you still feel that nature needs a bit of a helping hand, try K-Y Pessaries. Pop one inside you about ten minutes before intercourse and everything should be fine.

———

Q. I bought one of those new magazines for women that show pictures of nude men. It didn't turn me on a bit. Is there something wrong with me?

A. Well, if there is, there's something equally wrong with me and most other women I've talked to. I think the pics in those magazines are about as exciting as a plate of cold chipolatas!

Q. *I'm 19 and everybody says I'm sexy - but I know I'm a fraud.*

I have a great boyfriend, but I don't feel like a normal woman. You see I've never had an orgasm in my life. Can anything be done?

A. Very few women are born knowing how to reach orgasm. For most of us it's something that has to be learned, while for men it's much more instinctive.

The average age for a woman to start experiencing orgasms is shortly after her nineteenth birthday so you're not unusual at all.

My bet is that it won't be long before this happens to you.

But you can help yourself by learning how to do it alone first. Women who can masturbate to orgasm are in a much better position to show their partners what works for them.

Q. I like to think I'm a normal 20 year old, but one thing bothers me - I don't like sex very much. I've tried it many times - occasionally just for a quiet life - but the sex act has done nothing for me.

I can get quite excited kissing a guy and I even like having my breasts touched, but as soon as we get down to the real thing, I switch off.

Of course I wouldn't say I've been wildly in love with anyone yet. Also I tend not to go out with the same lad for very long. Do you think I should give them more of a chance? I feel I'm missing out.

A. You've been window-shopping with men so far, haven't you? You've wandered around sampling the merchandise, but you haven't felt like buying. There's nothing wrong with that.

Your sex urges are OK if you feel like kissing and caressing, but you probably, quite rightly, feel you can't let yourself go until you really care for someone. So don't invite anyone into your bed, or into your body, until you're sure you really like him. You don't have to offer yourself to some bloke just because he buys you a drink. But when you find a

likely candidate, do give him a proper chance. Remember that he may not move the earth for you the first time - after all, you'll both be nervous.

I feel quite confident that you'll grow to like sex, when you find the right man. And that means a man who really cares for you.

———

Q. I'm 23 and have just broken up with my boyfriend after four years. I've come off the Pill to give my system a rest, but I hope not to be alone for long.

I didn't worry much about AIDS when I was with my boyfriend, but now I'm definitely giving safe sex some thought. Does it look very forward if a woman carries her own condoms?

A. Forward or not - condoms can save your life as well as prevent unwanted pregnancies. Plenty of women have their own these days and there are now some called Ladymates in plain packets for women to carry without embarrassment.

Q. *My wife and I have been happily married for 25 years. The only problem is that as soon as I go to make love to her, she changes. It's as if she wants it over with as soon as possible. Obviously I'd like things to be different, but we don't talk about sex. I'm keen to try foreplay, but to tell you the truth, I haven't found her clitoris yet.*

A. Well, it's time you did! Sorry to be so blunt, but this is likely to be the all-important key to your wife's sexuality. Indeed, it's highly likely that your wife's lack of interest stems from your joint ignorance and lack of bedroom technique.

Here's a 3 point plan, but, before you embark on it, do reassure your wife that you love her and want to make her happy.

* Spend a romantic few hours leading up to love-making. Women can't just switch on a sexy mood like men can.
* For a list of excellent sex education books, send a large stamped addressed envelope to:- FPA, 27-35 Mortimer Street, London, W1N 7RJ.
* Buy *The Lovers' Guide* video. Watch it and experiment together.

Q. *A woman wrote to you recently to say that she hated her husband smacking her bottom. My problem is that I LOVE it.*

Some years ago I happened to see a boy spank his girl-friend's rear end when she had been flirting. This really turned me on. In fact I've never got it out of my system and recently I answered an ad in a magazine and got in touch with a man who humiliated me and spanked me all day until I was red raw. I thought that this had cured me, but now I want more.

A. For goodness sake, PLEASE don't answer any more ads like that one. Suppose the man had been even more peculiar - he could have killed you. No cheap thrill is worth that.

So do your best to find a decent guy who loves you. He might even give your bottom a little spanking from time to time, but hopefully you'll find that other types of love-play will excite you as much.

You don't have to go down this very dubious road. If you really can't rid yourself of these desires, have a chat with a woman doctor at your local Family Planning Clinic.

Q. I have a great boyfriend. We get on very well and have been living together since last July. He's wonderful in bed and it's through him that I've learned to enjoy sex. I'd never had an orgasm with a man before I met him, but now I often have them.

Sometimes though, when he finishes making love to me, even though I may have had an orgasm, I feel that I'm not satisfied. Then I tend to find it difficult to get to sleep, even though he's fast asleep beside me. Would it be too much to expect to have another climax or two?

A. Once a man has climaxed, he's not usually able to continue stimulating you with his penis for long, as he loses his erection and his energy quite quickly.

So it might be an idea to get him to give you more than one orgasm before he actually "comes" himself. But if this doesn't always work out, he can caress you afterwards with his fingers until you have another climax. Or, if he falls asleep, you can do it for yourself. Plenty of women do!

Q. Last week I saw a television programme about Readers' Wives. As I understand it, this is the name given to those women whose husbands and boyfriends send pictures of them to soft porn magazines.

I've always been a bit of a show-off and my husband has often taken saucy photos of me. So I suggested he send some of my pictures to those magazines. But he totally flipped his lid. He says he loves and worships my body and doesn't want other men looking at me. What do you think?

A. I'm with your husband on this one. Be thankful that he loves you and has such honour and respect for your body.

He knows that if your pictures are published, you'll be ogled by men of all types. He knows too that you could be embarrassed by remarks made by men you meet regularly - these magazines are read by teachers, milkmen, pub landlords, hairdressers ....

Many women would love to have a man who adores them in the way your husband does you.
So treasure your good relationship and don't risk spoiling it.

Q. *My latest boyfriend is older than me and much more sexually experienced. I like him, but he seems obsessed with my bottom. He likes to spank it when we're making love and sometimes this hurts. He also pinches my buttocks really hard. I think he'd like to do other things, but I don't want him to. I've never really liked my bottom and all this attention to it embarrasses and upsets me. What should I do?*

A. Many women grow up thinking that their bottoms are dirty, or too big, or just generally not very nice. And it often takes a loving, appreciative partner to help a woman realise that this part of her anatomy is not only OK, but also delights her partner into the bargain.

However NO-ONE should be engaging in any form of sex play that they don't like. And if what this man is doing, or trying to do, to you is just not your bag, then you must say so.

Maybe he's a bit old for you, or too way out. But whatever the reason, it's pointless being in a relationship that brings you more anxiety than joy.

Q. Why does everyone else think that sexual intercourse is so marvellous? I don't.

I'm 17 and I have been going out with my boyfriend for almost a year. We love each other very much and have been intimate together for several months. This has involved us touching and stimulating each other. He has orgasms when we do this, and I enjoy it a lot, though I'm not sure if I've had an orgasm or not.

But two months ago I went on the Pill and as soon as it was safe, we started having intercourse. My boyfriend thinks it's fantastic, but I'd sooner carry on doing what we did before. I found that much more exciting.

When we now have full sex I feel almost suffocated when my boyfriend lies on me and I don't have any pleasant feelings at all. I'm so fed up and don't know what to do.

A. If the two of you love each other and are prepared to experiment a bit, everything will improve, so cheer up.

For most men getting inside their partner is their top priority and it gives them marvellous sensations. But for many women the most exciting

feelings come from being stroked and stimulated. And even when they have full sex they need plenty of that kind of attention before intercourse and usually during it and afterwards as well. I don't suppose your boyfriend has realised this yet.

Also you should vary your sexual positions. Many girls prefer to climb on top themselves. They can control things better that way and feel freer without their man's weight on top of them.

As to your own orgasms, if you're not sure you've had one yet, you probably haven't. But the average age for a woman to start climaxing is 19, so time is on your side. Meanwhile the two of you could benefit from reading some good sex education books. The Family Planning Association has the best selection and you can buy them, without embarrassment, through mail order. Send a large stamped addressed envelope for their free catalogue to:- FPA Bookshop, 27-35 Mortimer Street, London, W1N 7RJ.

Difficult Family Situations

Show me a family and I'll show you a difficult situation. Perhaps that's over-stating the case, but MOST families go through terrific problems at some time or another and these can create terrible tension, days off work, truanting from school and genuine illnesses.

Of course most of us feel that we've failed if our family isn't happy, and we also tend to believe that everyone else copes with their children and their relatives wonderfully. Well, cheer up, because they don't. This next section should convince you.

Q. My 13 year old daughter is in love with a female teacher at her school. I couldn't cope if she turned out to be a lesbian.

A. It's much more likely that she just has a massive crush on this woman. Most young girls have a passion for someone of their own sex at sometime.

Don't ridicule your daughter. This is serious to her. But it's just a rehearsal for another kind of loving later on.

Q. I'm so glad that Christmas is over. It's been the worst ever and already I'm dreading the next one.

We've been married 12 years and every year we've gone to my wife's parents for the whole holiday. We go on Christmas Eve and stay until New Year's Day.

I shouldn't complain - it's just that I don't feel at home there. I can't even make love to my wife because the kids share our room. Everyone thinks I'm a nutcase, because I walk round their house opening windows all the time - even when it's freezing.

A. Trying to escape eh? You poor bloke. I reckon you deserve a medal, but it's time for a change.

For a start, are you sure that your in-laws enjoy having you all for so long? It's very hard work and tiring for older people to have their routine so completely disrupted.

I suggest that you tell your wife what you've told me. Be gentle and don't argue, but be firm. Then work out a compromise.

Perhaps you could cut down the visit to two or three days, or maybe your wife's parents could come to you for a change.

Another alternative would be for you and your wife to sleep at a bed and breakfast place near your in-laws, so that at least you'd have a haven for the two of you at the end of each day and could enjoy a spot of Yuletide nookie.

You've got 12 months to work this out. I'm sure you can and maybe everyone else will be relieved that you've had the courage to speak out. Good luck!

———

Q. *There was a letter on your page recently from a young man hoping to contact his long-lost father. I wish it had been from my boy, I lost touch with him after my ex-wife re-married, as her husband didn't like me contacting the kids. Could I get in touch with them now?*

A. You should try. It's important for children of divorced people to know that both parents love them. An organisation called Families Need Fathers will help you. Ring: 081-886-0970.

Q. My younger sister and I share a small flat. She's a very happy-go-lucky kind of person, whereas I've always been more serious.

I've got a much better job than her and it takes up all my energy. I'm engaged to an army sergeant who's away a lot of the time. My sister has a couple of men on the go and often brings one or other of them home to spend the night.

She's very loud and the racket from their love-making keeps me awake in the next room. Do you think she HAS to make so much noise?

A. Frankly I think your relationship with your sister is highly competitive. Perhaps she minds that you're engaged and that you have a better job. Maybe she wants you to envy her love life.

Still, you need your sleep. Be thankful you're sharing with a sister rather than a friend: it should be easier to tell a relation that you can't tolerate her bedroom habits. Persuade her that even the most passionate of people can muffle their ecstasy. Suggest she bites on the pillow!

Q. *I'm in love with two very nice women - but they are* MOTHER *and* DAUGHTER.

There's only eighteen years between them, and in many ways they seem like sisters. When I visit them, I have a wonderful time. In fact as soon as I arrive they're so ready for sex that they're tearing their clothes off.

The point is that Mum wants a baby by me. But is she too old at 48? And if she is, should the daughter and I try for a family?

A. The answer to your first question is yes, and my answer to the second is a resounding NO.

What you have going for you wouldn't be everybody's cup of tea, but it's obvious the three of you are enjoying it. You don't say whether you all leap into bed together or whether you romance your women one at a time. But I'm sure many men reading this will admire your stamina!

Babies are something else though. And a horrible thought has just struck me that you might manage to get BOTH these women pregnant at the same time. What a complicated set of family relationships THAT would produce!

I reckon it would be disastrous to introduce a baby into your threesome. Your cosy triangle would undoubtedly suffer and I can only guess at the damage to a child growing up in such a weird set-up.

———

Q. Please can you help as my whole family is very upset. You see, my brother is living with my sister's daughter - that is to say, his niece. Apart from a huge age difference, surely this is illegal?

A. Sometimes people who shouldn't fall in love DO fall in love. That's life. But of course it's enormously difficult for the rest of the family.

My answer may surprise you. Your brother and his niece are NOT breaking the law. Amazing, isn't it? But I'm assured by a police superintendent that this is the case.

However this country's laws forbid marriage between them. And I hope they know that having children would be very dodgy indeed. With a bit of luck this weird love affair will burn itself out. But if it doesn't, I hope the rest of you will try to come round to the idea. Family rifts are usually not only painful, but pointless in the end.

———————

Q. *The other day I was tidying up my husband's wardrobe when I found a bag containing nappies, bibs, a dummy and feeding bottle.*

I was totally shocked. I have read about men who get turned on by play-acting that they're babies, but I've never had the remotest suspicion that my husband was this kind of pervert. I feel quite sick and don't know whether or not to talk to him about this. What do you think?

A. I'm desperately sorry you had to make this discovery. In fact this kind of habit is quite common. Maybe your husband felt safe as a child and chooses to dress up to re-create those happy times. He may be content with things as they are, so it's up to you whether you challenge him about it. Though I can't help wondering if he left his bag of tricks where you would find it in the hope of bringing things out into the open. He may even want you to be part of his fantasy and hope that you'll cuddle him, feed or even change him.

It's hard to advise you what to do, except to say please take things very slowly. If your marriage is to survive, you'll need to retain respect for your husband and playing these games with him might destroy that for good.

———————

Q. My son had a relationship with a really bossy girl for eight years during which time they had two children. Now they've split up, but he still lets her walk all over him. She's got another man at the moment, but I sometimes think she might tire of him and come crawling back to my son. What can I do?

A. Nothing! It's not fair being a parent, is it? Children don't stop getting themselves into messes just because they're supposed to be grown up. The hardest thing for parents to learn is that their childrens' romantic partnerships are NOTHING to do with them. Your job is to help and support your son, no matter what you think of the situation.

———

Q. My husband has beaten me up throughout our marriage. We split up once, but ended up staying in the same house as I had nowhere else to go.

After that he raped me while my daughter was going hysterical in the same room.

I'm sure he sees at least one other woman, but when I complain, he calls me stupid.

I don't want my kids to think that violence is the norm - my husband sometimes even threatens them when they get on his nerves. I don't want to split up. I just want help. Please print this as I dare not receive a private reply.

A. Heaven only knows why you want to stay with someone who treats you more like a slave than a wife. I can only assume it must be OK some of the time.

Apart from your own injuries, like you, I'm worried about the effect all this is having on your kids. Please talk to an expert. Ring the Womens' Aid National Helpline on 0272-633542.

Q. *My problem may seem a little odd, but I think you may be able to help me to sort it out.*

I was on my own for several years after a bitter divorce. Now I've re-married and I think that this time I'm going to be lucky.

My new wife is a wonderful person in every way. The only difficulty is that I have two children who come to visit me every weekend and when they're in the house, I don't feel able to make love to my wife.

She's very understanding, but I'm sure she must feel hurt as I'm all over her the rest of the time.

A. Maybe she's glad of the rest! Seriously, give her lots of reassurance and love at weekends. Often women are even more delighted to have that than to be engaged in real sex. Don't forget though that weekends with your kids are probably quite an ordeal for your wife too - there's no training course that prepares you for becoming a step-parent. When the children and the two of you are more used to each other and your new situation, I'm sure that normal services will be resumed!

———————

Q. I've been sleeping with my boyfriend for almost a year and I've just discovered that I'm pregnant. We're both 18 and both sets of parents assume we'll get married.

But I'm not sure I want to spend the rest of my life with this boy. I want to get a job and I want to travel and do things. I'm not keen on abortion and don't think I could go through with that. Do you think I could get the baby adopted?

A. If only you'd realised how much you value your independence BEFORE an innocent baby was on the way. However I think you'd be mad to go through with marriage, feeling as you do. It'll take a lot of courage to swim against the tide here, but it'll definitely be better than marrying the wrong man.

I think you're right not to consider abortion since you obviously have real reservations about it. I'm always getting letters from women who bitterly regret having terminated their babies.

Adoption is a good option. There are ten times more couples WANTING to adopt than there are babies. So I'm sure your baby will be deeply loved and wanted. If you'd like the child to be adopted through any agency in particular, please drop me another line and I'll put you in touch with them.

———————

Q. I was an unhappy little girl. My dad picked on me and often beat me. I don't know why he singled me out - he never touched my sisters. Fortunately I met and married a wonderful man whose family treat me as one of their own. My parents didn't come to our wedding and have rarely seen my children, who are 7 and 10. Why won't my parents accept me and be grandparents to my kids?

A. I wish I could tell you. But in my opinion your parents should come to you on bended knees, begging for forgiveness. I'm amazed that you still want to see them at all. Make one last attempt. Get your children to write notes to Granny and Grandad inviting them for a visit. If they don't respond, I hope you'll stop torturing yourself and write them off.

———

Q. *My wife and I are very happily married with a great sex life. Three months ago we had our first baby. I've always wanted to be a dad, so I was really chuffed. The baby's perfect except for one thing. Although he's good during the day, he turns into a monster at night. Every night it's the same, he screams and cries for hours. This is doing nothing for our sex life, I can tell you.*

We took him to the doctor, but he didn't even bother to examine him. His attitude seemed to be that the baby would grow out of it and we just had to lump it. My poor wife looks terrible due to lack of sleep. I try to do my share, but I need my rest and, as I've just been promoted, I'm worried that I won't be able to keep up with my work.

A. Well, for a start, I should consider changing your doctor.

Attitudes like his make my blood boil. It should have been obvious to him that the whole family is suffering, and also that, if things don't improve, your health and your marriage might suffer. So take your baby for a second opinion, even if it's within the same practice. There probably isn't anything wrong with him, but you need to have your minds put at rest.

Next, try to get a friend or relative to give your wife a break in the daytime. If she could have a long sleep in the afternoon, she would at least feel a bit more human.

Then contact CRYSIS. It's an organisation for parents like you whose babies keep crying. It would do you good to talk with other parents who've had the same trouble. Ring them on: 071-404-5011.

Q. *I've been living with my boyfriend for a year and we get on well.*

The only problem is that his children from his first marriage, aged 5 and 8, come and stay at weekends.

Whatever I ask them to do, they do the opposite. It's causing arguments and their father always takes their side. We can't go on like this.

A. The children are behaving badly, it's true. But they may feel that nobody wants them - no wonder they're naughty. The harsh truth is that you are grown-up, and they're not, so it's up to you to solve the problem.

Make sure that they have a room, or at least an area in your house that they can call their own. Visiting children are often disruptive simply because they don't have any of their toys or books around them. So encourage the kids to keep some of their favourite things at your place and that way they'll be more likely to think of it as their second home.

You should also ensure that they understand how much you love their father; and that you're planning to stick around. It's important to spell this out. There have been many changes in these kids' lives and they may think you're a temporary fixture and therefore not worth bothering about.

Think up things to do with them at weekends. Once they sense that you're pleased to see them, and not just putting up with them, I'm sure they'll respond.

And once your man sees how much you're trying with his kids, I'm sure he'll agree that there need to be some house rules. These could include what time the kids should go to bed and what areas they should keep tidy. Once these rules are drawn up, you should support each other over them, and keep them.

The step-family situation is fraught with difficulty, but your future with this man depends on your success with his kids. They're not going to stop being part of his life, so you need to regard them as friends. Call the Stepfamily Association on: 071-372-0846 for further help.

Q. *My eldest daughter has been having a relationship with a man I can only describe as an ANIMAL. They've been together for ten years and have a boy of 5. This man has tried to kill my daughter. I called the police, but when the case came to court, she felt sorry for him and denied everything.*

Since then he's tried to strangle her, he's broken her hand and covered her in bruises.
She has a 15 year old son from a previous marriage who's threatened to run away. And the 5 year old, who is the son of this beast, is desperately unhappy.

We're all terrified of this maniac and I live in dread that my daughter will be murdered.

A. Unless your daughter makes a stand, your hands are tied. If she won't support your complaints to the police, they're a waste of time. If you could persuade her to call the Women's Aid National Helpline on 0272-633542 that would be a good start. Otherwise, concentrate on your poor, frightened grandchildren. Call the NSPCC 24 hour free helpline on: 0800-800500.

Q. *I'm 18 and the only member of my family who has been to college. My mum and dad are both proud of me.*

The problem is that I'm meeting lots of new friends from quite different backgrounds. Some are vegetarian and others hold views that my dad would never understand.

Also I now have a boyfriend, but his family is very different from mine.

It's not that I'm ashamed of my background, it's just that I can't imagine inviting my boyfriend or any of my other friends home.

A. REAL friends will see your home for what it is - a decent, ordinary place with good, sound values.

Be proud of your family. It's their sacrifices that have given you the chance of a better life. Of course you're learning things that your family can't share, but it would be cruel to make your dad feel uneducated and inadequate in his own home. So if you and he no longer see eye to eye on certain issues, just button your lip until you can afford a place of your own.

Q. *I've got a 15 year old sister. I'm 21. She came to my flat the other day in floods of tears saying she's pregnant by her boyfriend. She won't tell mum and dad and wants me to arrange an abortion for her. But I don't want to take this responsibility. Also I'm worried that my mum will blame me if it ever comes out. I'm sure mum would agree to her having an abortion, because she thinks anything is better than young girls bringing unwanted kids into the world. But I'm still worried about deceiving her. What would you suggest?*

A. Obviously if your parents were likely to throw your sister out there would be a huge problem. But that doesn't sound likely. So I think you should persuade your sister to tell your mother the truth. Or maybe YOU should tell her, with your sister's consent. Though mum will probably be shocked and disappointed, I'm sure she'll quickly buckle down to this crisis and deal with it.

I know that your sister is upset and frightened, but she considered herself old enough to have sex, and now, I'm afraid, she must learn that she's old enough to face the consequences. In my opinion, asking you to arrange a secret abortion is unfair, and too much for you to take on.

Q. I'm so miserable I just had to write to you. I feel that everyone in the world has had a great Christmas except me. I spent the whole time alone watching the telly and eating boring food out of cans. I didn't have anything special at all. I suppose I could have gone to my mum, but we would only have ended up arguing. My sister and I don't get on and my dad is divorced from my mum and I don't like his new family.

Worst of all my boyfriend gave me up last November. He was my whole life - I didn't do anything unless he was around. Now he's gone my life is empty.

I have a job, thank goodness, but other than that my life is awful. Please can you help?

A. I'm sorry you're miserable, but I must put you right on one or two things. The whole of the rest of the world did NOT have a wonderful Christmas. For lots of people Christmas is a difficult and lonely time. And even for those surrounded by loving families, it's a frantic time and one that demands a lot of compromise.

I know two women who were divorced last year. Like you they dreaded Christmas. But unlike you, they worked in an old folk's home over the holiday. They reacted positively.

But you're negative about most things and you blame others for everything that happens to you. This isn't realistic. You have to grow up and start taking responsibility for yourself.

I expect your boyfriend loved you, but couldn't cope with your expectations that HE would make you happy all the time. Did you ever take him out for a meal? Or give him a surprise outing? I doubt it.

Your family probably love you too, but I bet they're sick to death of your attitude. You don't have to go through life like this.

Why not make a New Year's resolution to get out and do new things and make new friends. Take an evening class in something you're interested in. Learn to cook properly and invite a colleague to your flat for supper. Life will pass you by unless you start putting something into it.

Q. Twenty years ago my mate and his girlfriend broke up. I "comforted" the girl for a while, but then the two of them made it up and got married. We stayed friends, but later I married and moved away and we lost touch.

Last week that couple's first child - a daughter, who's now 19 -turned up and told me that she believes I'm her father. Although it was a shock, I wasn't totally surprised. I remember being fascinated by her when she was small. Apparently she's discussed all this with her parents. They've agreed that she's mine and fortunately there are no hard feelings.

But now she wants to know me better. However, I'm worried that my wife and children may not be able to accept this news. What can I do?

A. Tell your "daughter" gently that you need some time to come to terms with this bolt from the blue. Then find a good moment to discuss it with your wife. It'll be a shock, but I'm sure she'll realise that such things happen, and that your fling was over YEARS before the two of you met. With luck she'll understand your desire to get to know the girl and will feel able to invite her to your home in time.

Q. *My dad re-married last year. The woman is a lot younger and frankly I didn't think she was suitable. But dad's besotted with her and is very happy.*

I'm married, but my 17 year old brother lives with dad. Several times when I've been round there recently I've thought that dad's wife is paying my brother too much attention. She teases him and keeps touching his arm. It worries me what might go on while I'm not around. My brother's fallen totally under her spell - she's a very bubbly person. But I feel worried. It would be awful if dad got hurt.

A. It's obvious that you don't like the woman and this makes me wonder if you're imagining trouble where it doesn't exist. But if your suspicions are correct, then something must be done to protect your dad. So keep an eye on brother and "stepmum," and if you're still worried in a few weeks, tackle your brother. Young men of that age tend to blush easily and you should be able to guess if anything untoward is going on. If it IS, you should warn the lady that you've sussed her little game. I'm sure she doesn't want her marriage to end prematurely, so let's hope she'll mend her ways and be sensible.

Q. *I'm a man of 23. I've always been appalled by stories of parents being violent towards their kids. But the other day our baby was screaming and screeching - he was teething - and I had a headache. Without thinking I picked him up and shook him hard. Then I realised what I'd done. Thank God he seemed to be all right, but I'm terrified now that I might really hurt him another time.*

I thought we'd enjoy having a child. But so far it's been no fun at all. What shall I do?

A. You WILL have fun with your little boy, when he's a bit older and you can do things with him. But in the meantime, like lots of young parents, you're tired and stressed and not yet used to the disruption a baby causes.

Violence can never be excused, especially towards a defenceless baby. But many parents feel they're reaching the end of their tether when their infants seem to do nothing but cry, so you're not alone. Call Parentline on: 0268-757077. They'll understand, and do what they can to help.

Q. *I got a divorce last year after a miserable marriage. My husband was a womaniser and he also wanted more sex from me than I could cope with. I grew to hate him.*

But my two children, who are 12 and 10, love their dad. I've had to agree to him seeing them at weekends, but I dread it. I resent him seeing them when he's such an awful person. All the time they're away I feel unable to think of anything else. If they were younger I might be able to talk them out of seeing him, but there's no chance now that they're this age. What can I do?

A. You must change your attitude. You and your ex had your differences, but your children are as much his as they are yours. If you put pressure on them NOT to see him, you might end up a very lonely woman. Your kids will resent any interference and in time may rule YOU out of their lives, not HIM.

Do something positive at weekends - see friends or family, take up a hobby or even catch up on your sleep. That way you should mind less that the kids are away.

Q. *I've been seeing my boyfriend for two years. I'm 35 and was divorced three years ago after a dreadful marriage.*

My boyfriend has never been married, although he has had girlfriends. He's 33.

We go out together twice a week and on those evenings he sleeps with me. Our sex life isn't very exciting, but it's OK. My boyfriend is a gentle man, quite unlike my ex-husband who wanted a lot of very odd sex.

But now I'd like our relationship to develop - possibly into marriage - and I've suggested that we live together.

But my boyfriend says he can't leave his mother alone - she's a widow and he's an only child.

I know she doesn't like me, so although I love this man, I can't help wondering if he'll ever be mine. Do you think I ought to cut my losses now while I'm hopefully still young enough to find someone else?

A. It's time you two had a long chat. You know what YOU want - a new husband, love and security. Does HE know that? And, more importantly, does he want the same things? He may not.

Clearly he's very attached to his mum and he doesn't appear to have a great sex drive. So maybe the combination of mum's cooking and company plus your occasional sexual favours are his idea of heaven. I'm afraid it sounds to me as if he could enjoy this situation for ever.

You say his mum doesn't like you. I doubt if she'd be keen on ANYONE in your place. She almost certainly wants to keep her boy for herself.

So ask your man what he wants. If he claims to love you, then insist that he spends more time with you. You can hardly judge what living together would be like while you see each other so rarely.

But if he shies away from any more commitment, you'll have to accept that he's a mummy's boy and either put up with it, or get yourself back into circulation.

Q. I have a daughter of 8. To my amazement one of her friends is already developing breasts. I still think of my kid as a baby. But this has made me realise she's growing up fast.

Will the school teach her about periods and sex? I'd feel very shy about having to do it myself.

A. Sex education varies enormously from school to school let alone between different parts of the country and I certainly don't think you can bank on her being given any useful information for a couple of years or so.

Obviously she'll need to know things before then. Kids are fascinated by sex and I bet she's already picked up some half-baked theories in the playground.

I suggest you get a useful little pamphlet called *Answering Your Kids' Questions - Information for Parents*. It costs £1.50 (including postage and packing) from:- The FPA, 27-35 Mortimer Street, London, W1N 7RJ.

Q. *I'm 24. Recently I met a girl I really like and I'm wondering if she's "the one."*

I'd like to marry and have kids. But I'm bothered by the fact that I come from a big, close family, while my girlfriend is an only child of much older parents.

She can't understand the relationship I have with my parents and brothers and resents the time I spend with them. She doesn't get on with her parents and never mentions any cousins or aunts or anything. Do you think these differences would matter if we married?

A. **They may. What's even more important is whether her view on children coincides with yours. Does she want them if she's so self-contained? And would she be prepared for them to mix in with your extended family - I'm sure this would be very important to you.**

You're right to be wary. Issues like this do matter, and unless you can resolve them, I think you'd be unwise to think of marriage.

Q. When dad died suddenly last year, my sister and I had mum round to our homes as often as possible. In fact she had at least one meal a day either in my sister's house or mine.

Now, ten months after dad's death, mum still comes to one of us every day. It's become very difficult. My children resent the fact that they can't watch the programmes they want on television or have their friends in, and my husband is fed-up too.

Life at my sister's is no better. What can we do?

A. Your mum is probably still shocked by your dad's death. And maybe she finds being home alone is very painful for her. Perhaps you and your sister could go round there sometimes rather than have her visit you. And try discussing with her what she wants to do with her life now. Also give her the chance to talk about your dad, and if she wants to have a good cry - let her. It would also be useful to put her in touch with CRUSE, the association for the bereaved - the number will be in your local phone book.

Next, to keep both your families happy, you'll need to find a way of limiting mum's visits. So give her a schedule of when you can see her and when you can't. Be firm about this, but make sure that she can always get you on the phone on days she doesn't see you. Also ensure that she is in no doubt about when she may visit again.

It might also be helpful to encourage her to make more friends amongst her neighbours. There will almost certainly be other elderly folk living alone nearby.

Once there is more space between visits I'm sure your kids will be more welcoming when gran turns up. I hope so - it's no fun being old and lonely.

It's early days, so try not to despair. I'm sure if you follow these suggestions, your mum will gradually become more independent.

Affairs

Affairs make up a large section of any agony aunt's postbag.

At the beginning of any affair there's always excitement and hope. There's usually some pretty abandoned sex too and plenty of romantic encounters.

But affairs HURT. Nearly always they damage at least one person badly. And often all the parties involved suffer terrible heartache.

Q. I have the most wonderful man - except for one thing. He's still married to someone else. He sees me regularly, including Christmas and my birthday, but he always leaves half-way through the night to go back to his wife.

What can I do to make him come to me full time?

A. Not very much, I'm afraid. When a man has got two women eager to look after him, he has no real reason to face the upheaval of a divorce.

So, you have to make a decision. Will you stay with him, even if he <u>never</u> leaves his wife? Many women who love their men do agree to this, even though they're certain to suffer terrible loneliness. If you can't face a future like this, then you should end the affair. And that's what I hope you'll do.

Q. *My wife can't stop having affairs with other men. She says that they don't matter to her, but that she just needs a bit of a buzz in her life.*

I was attracted to her because she was so outgoing, and I was amazed that she settled with me, as I thought she'd have wanted someone more exciting. But she insists she can't live without me. However I can't cope with her affairs - they're leaving me gutted.

A. Your wife says she can't live without you. It's time to test that out. Tell her you won't stay with her unless she stops the affairs. If she agrees, romance her and keep your love life brimful of passion. But if she won't, I think you'll have to part. But I'm sure a nice guy like you won't be on your own for long.

Q. I've been living with my man for 10 years. Although we're not married, we have children and I thought that we were happy and settled.

Unfortunately my cosy world has collapsed. My bloke had to go away to work and his contract won't end till the autumn. I now have proof that he's been seeing another woman while he's away. I found a note from her.

My boyfriend swears there's nothing in it. He says this lady has fallen on hard times after being treated badly by her ex-husband. He insists he's only being friendly and they only have an occasional drink. If I left him, it would mean the kids and me losing our home. Also, my eldest really adores her dad.

My man is desperate at how upset I've been. He rings me every night and keeps telling me he doesn't want to live without me. But I can't sleep. I'm edgy with the children and I feel wretched and rejected.

A. First things first. You only have proof that your bloke sees another woman for an occasional drink. This doesn't necessarily mean that he's having an affair. He may genuinely be trying to cheer up this poor soul. He may even have been having a drink

with her to cheer HIMSELF up. Working away from home can be very lonely.

Whatever happened, I think he's trying to tell you in every possible way how much he loves and needs you and the children. So please don't split up over this. I'm sure you'd regret it.

Try instead to concentrate on all the good things in your life, then I suggest you:-

* Give him a warm and wonderful welcome every time he comes home.
* Arrange for you and the kids to visit him next week during half term.
* Hang on in there until he finishes this job. I bet he's longing for it to end as much as you are.

Q. *Geoff and I have been married for five years. We have no children and although I'm not the lovey-dovey type, we don't argue much. He stays away on business once a week. I don't mind that at all, but now I've discovered that he's been having an affair.*

You see, he started washing his own shirts and underwear as soon as he came home. But this week I got to his bag before he did. His shirt collar was covered in lipstick and there were sex stains lower down on the shirt and on his underpants.

I haven't spoken to him yet, as I'm sure he'll be devastated that I've found out.

I think I love him. And I certainly have no wish to start again on my own.

A. I understand that you don't want to be on your own. But if that's your MAIN reason for keeping the marriage going, I'm afraid I don't see much future for it. And I have to say the strong impression I gain from your letter is that your relationship is a long way from being the passion of the century.

You obviously believe that Geoff has been trying to keep his affair from you. But I don't agree. In fact I think he's been VERY keen to tell you. So much so that I'm surprised he didn't paint "I'm being unfaithful" on a hoarding outside your house.

If he hadn't wanted to arouse your suspicions, he'd have gone to a launderette with his dirty washing. And I bet there have been other clues left lying round the place: it's just that you haven't wanted to spot them.

What you must do now is to analyse your marriage.

My guess is that you are much less interested in sex than your husband and that this has been a problem for him. Are you prepared to talk this out? And if I'm right, are you prepared to work something out between you? Maybe you can't change your nature and the fairest thing for you both would be to split, so that you can both find partners who are more compatible sexually.

But Geoff's affair has provided you with a chance to talk about and then work on your less than perfect marriage.

If you both want to make it work, make an appointment at Relate and start trying to understand each other better.

Q. *Recently I slept with my best friend's boyfriend after they had a row.*

I enjoyed it and didn't feel guilty as my friend never found out. But the next day she visited me and my two kids to tell me how much she loves him. Now they're back together and I can't bear it. It's tough because we all drink at the same pub and I feel nothing but hate and jealousy towards her. I don't know what to do.

A. I'm glad I don't have a friend like you! Just be grateful that your girlfriend hasn't found out yet that you slept with her man.

I should avoid your local and the usual drinking crowd and investigate some clubs or groups in your area where you could meet other people. I get the feeling you're prepared to use sex to get company. But please don't - it's far too important for that.

You need your own man - someone who will love you for what you are - so start looking for him and stop hankering after your friend's bloke.

Q. I wish I could get my ex-husband back. We got divorced after I had an affair. I thought I was mad about my lover, but it all went wrong and my life is in tatters.

My ex is now seeing someone else and they're talking about buying a house together, although she's not divorced yet.

When my former husband comes to see the kids I feel like dragging him in and taking him to bed. But he won't come into the house. Now I just can't get him out of my mind and it's driving me mad.

A. Yours is a very sorry tale, my love, and one that I hear all too frequently. What a pity you allowed yourself to have an affair before you realised how important your husband was to you.

I'm sure he was horribly hurt by your rejection and it's not surprising that he's sought comfort elsewhere.

Part of me wonders whether you're simply jealous now that your husband has managed to find happiness with another woman. However, if you think your feelings are genuine, why not write a love

letter to your husband, admitting your mistakes and asking for a second chance.

I'm not sure he'll give you one, but if he does, do make sure that you shower him will all the love you should have shown him before.

———

Q. *My wife and I have been together for four years and we have two small children. Our sex life used to be great and we would make love at least four times a week. Now it's hardly at all.*

I try to help with the kids and also to make my wife feel appreciated by buying her sexy underwear and so on. But nothing works. And when we occasionally have sex, she just lies there. Now I'm seriously thinking about having an affair.

A. Part of you wants me to say, "Go ahead, have an affair, you deserve it." While another part wants me to forbid you to stray. I can't do either in this terribly sad, but all too common situation.

I believe you when you say you've tried everything to show your wife you value her. But I suspect she's not well and that she's depressed after the birth of your second child. She needs help and understanding, so please don't betray her.

Get someone to look after the kids for a weekend so that the two of you can go away and talk things through together. You may be able to impress upon her how much a young man like yourself needs sex and maybe come to some sort of compromise where she'll give you sexual relief by hand and will cuddle you, on condition that you don't try to penetrate her until she's ready and feels more like it. But even if she can't cope with that, I'm sure that you'd both benefit from some holding and getting really close.

In addition get her to visit her doctor. He or she may be able to give some helpful advice or medication. I also suggest that you contact the Meet-A-Mum Association, which is for post-natally depressed women. Send a large stamped addressed envelope to:- 58 Malden Road, South Norwood, London, SE25 4HS.

Affairs tend to lead to divorce, which is a bitter and final step, so please try to keep your marriage going, instead of taking a step that might wreck your life.

Q. My marriage was going through a dull patch a year ago so I had a one-night stand with someone at work. I didn't enjoy it one bit and felt like a slut afterwards.

Then I realised how decent and hard-working my husband is and how much I really loved him.

But some time later, I realised I was pregnant. My pregnancy was a nightmare, as I felt sure the child would turn out to be my colleague's child. I had a son, and my husband is on cloud nine. He keeps saying how much the baby is like him and, to tell you the truth, I'm beginning to see the resemblance myself. But do you think I should confess my unfaithfulness?

A. No. Since you only had sex once with the other man, and the baby looks like your husband, there's a VERY strong possibility that your husband is the father.

In any event, he's so happy with his baby, I think it would break his heart if he learned of your infidelity. I'm sure you have a good marriage and you won't stray in the future. So put the past behind you. You've suffered enough. And if you need to confess to someone, see a priest, minister or doctor.

———

Q. After my mate's marriage broke up I let him stay with us. Now he's repaid my kindness by running off with my wife. I'm left with our three children, while she lives the life of a love-sick teenager in a bed-sit with this bloke.

She's even talking about getting a house with him, although I can't see how they'll manage, as he doesn't have a job. I don't want to be forced into a divorce and I'm sure she'll soon tire of him as he's a real womaniser. If only she would agree to talk with me. I just want her back.

A. Perhaps your wife felt there was no romance in her life. Your mate probably gives her that, for the time being. But he sounds a rat who is unlikely to keep any woman happy long-term.

Don't rush into a divorce - you don't have to. Write and tell her what she means to you. Then propose a meeting somewhere that has romantic memories for both of you. If you can get her to see how much you love her and also what happiness she's throwing away, there's a good chance she'll come back.

———

Q. I've been married for ten years. Eight years ago my husband had an affair. I found out and was deeply upset.

He was sorry that he'd hurt me and gave up the other woman. But I know that he loved her - he still talks about her in his sleep.

Obviously I was pleased that he came back to me and we've tried to make our marriage work, but it's not great. And sometimes I've felt mean because I know I've held on to my husband just for the sake of our nine year old son and for security. I don't love or want HIM and I'm sure he knows it.

Now the tables have turned and I've fallen in love with a wonderful man. He'd like to marry me and I long to be with him.

I now see that my husband and I have NEVER had this kind of relationship and realise what it must have been like for him to truly love someone else.

He sacrificed his great love for our marriage. Must I do the same?

A. You don't say how old you are but my bet is that you're still in your early thirties. So the prospect of the two of you continuing to struggle with this empty marriage is a pretty gloomy one.

It's time you and your husband had a heart to heart. He's clearly a decent bloke and maybe he'll be relieved finally to talk about his hopes and dreams and about how they haven't been fulfilled by you. I can't help wondering if his lover is still around and keen on him - that would make a nice, tidy and happy solution.

But whether or not this is the case, be honest with your husband about your great love. I doubt if he'll want you to go through the pain of parting that he had to endure. Especially when your marriage is such a diluted version of what it should be.

Divorce is rarely amicable, but I've a feeling it might come as something of a relief to both of you. But just remember that your child loves both of you and has done nothing to deserve all this upset. So please make sure that he's considered properly when any major decisions are taken.

———————

Q. I've been having an affair with my girlfriend for three years. She's wonderful in bed - much keener on sex than my wife - and we get on well in every other way.

I've never made promises to her about leaving home as I'm fond of my wife and she's a good partner and mother - we've got kids of 5 and 8.

I'd hate to split up my home and I'm sure that if I DID leave, my wife would take me to the cleaners.

But now my girlfriend is getting restless. She's always going on about being with me full time. Then yesterday she said she's sick of sitting around hoping I'll turn up and is planning a summer holiday abroad with a whole group of people.

I've asked her to be faithful to me, as I couldn't bear it if she weren't. Also I'd be worried that she might catch something which I might pass on to my wife.

We have such a good life together, why won't she leave things as they are. Please help. I'm terrified of losing her.

A. I bet you are. To say you're having your cake and eating it would be this year's understatement.

Your girlfriend has had enough. She's spent three years surviving on the crumbs of your company, never knowing when she might see you. She's spent Christmases, New Years, birthdays and summer holidays alone, because you're always with your wife.

Now she's in effect giving you an ultimatum - come to her, or risk losing her. Let me tell you I hope she goes on this holiday, has a ball and never gives you a second thought. You're a selfish rat and it's time you realised that the world doesn't revolve around you.

Count yourself lucky too that, so far, no one has told your wife about your affair. You could lose everything - money, wife, children AND girlfriend if you're not careful. So start putting some proper energy into your marriage. Make your wife and family the top priority in your life and use some of the sexual techniques you've learned with your lover to liven up the marriage bed. You have to give up your lover, of course, but don't worry... she'll be much better off without you.

———

Q. I've lived with my partner for five years and we have two children.

Last year I was stunned when he told me that he'd met someone else and was leaving. He said he and this woman were deeply in love.

Our relationship is not a good one, but I didn't want him to quit as I'd be worse off financially if he walked out. To make him stay, I told him I wouldn't let him see the kids if he went. He adores them - and that did the trick.

Now, a year later, I've found out that he never gave up the other woman. So, should I let him go? I know there is no hope left for our relationship.

A. It's very frightening for a woman to be left on her own, especially when she's worried about money. But it's worse to tie someone to you when you know he just can't wait to get away.

I think you're right in saying that your relationship is over. I also believe that your partner's other romance must be incredibly strong to have survived all this trauma.

It also sounds as if the other woman loves your man for himself, and NOT just his pay packet.

Frankly I think your existence with your partner is now pointless. Also, you're unlikely to meet someone else while you're stuck in this rut.

So my advice would be to consider letting your man go. But ask about legal help at your local Citizens' Advice Bureau first.

Divorce

People frequently believe that they can get divorced without hurt and bitterness. Sadly they're generally mistaken. I don't know anyone who's come through a divorce who would want to repeat the experience.

Still, many folk feel mightily relieved when a bad marriage is over, even though they're usually worse off financially and often lonely.

But freshly divorced people are vulnerable. They sometimes get into new relationships far too quickly, just to prove they're still attractive. And they can feel very unhappy. Here are some letters that are typical of divorced peoples' problems.

———

Q. Is there an organisation for divorced people? I'm a man of 35 and I've been very lonely since my wife left.

A. Try Solo Clubs. Send a large stamped addressed envelope to: Room 8, Ruskin Chambers, 191 Corporation Street, Birmingham B4 6RY.

Q. *Since my marriage broke up two years ago, I've been on my own. My divorce is soon to become final and I'd like to get out and about again.*

The trouble is that my wife told me that I was very unattractive. She went on and on about it. Now when I look in the mirror, I don't like what I see. Also my confidence was badly shaken by my wife leaving in the first place.

A. Everyone's confidence is knocked by a divorce. It's a miserable time and most folk feel they're going to be alone for ever. In fact few people are!

Your wife sounds incredibly vindictive. It sounds to me as if she had to pretend to herself that you were ugly, just so she wouldn't feel guilty about leaving.

But many women want to believe that their discarded husbands are hopeless and that no-one else will want them. When such husbands meet other ladies, their ex-wives are frequently furious.

So take a long look at yourself. If you've let yourself go - put things right. But then forget about your first wife and her problems. Just get back into the world and start the rest of your life.

Q. My miserable marriage is over. I'm getting a divorce and I've met a lovely man who seems keen to spend time with me.

But he won't come to my house. He says he doesn't want anyone to connect him with the divorce. And he certainly wants to avoid ruining my reputation.

I couldn't care less myself. Why is he like this?

A. Be grateful that he's such a gent. You're impatient to start your new life, which is understandable. But this man is not responsible for your divorce and he doesn't want anyone to think that he is - you must respect this.

He also wants you to be blameless in the eyes of your neighbours. So be patient and go along with his wishes. You'll be glad you did in the end.

Q. Two years ago my wife and I were going through a very bad patch. I was working too hard and she was bored. Stupidly we let ourselves get talked into a wife swap with a couple of neighbours.

At first it seemed just the ticket. We had a bit of excitement and our own sex life seemed to improve as a result.

But then my wife fell for the other guy and said she wanted to live with him. We divorced and I set up house with the other woman. She's a very sexy lady, but I've never loved her as I did my own wife.

My wife and her bloke moved to the other side of town, but after a while she started ringing me up and we'd sneak off for a coffee or a drink.

Last week she threw herself into my arms and said she wanted us to get back together. I'd like to agree, but what about the other couple? They're divorced too. And then there are our kids to consider. They're just getting used to their new lives.

A. It's time you took a decision. Yes, YOU! You seem to have fallen in with everyone else's plans just for a quiet life.

What do YOU want to do? Are you still in love with your wife? Is your wife really in love with you? Or is she now just a bit bored with the other chap?

If the two of you are convinced that you're meant to be together, I'm sure your kids will be delighted. It's very rare for children to be pleased that their parents have split.

As for the other couple, they started all this and they'll just have to cope with the upheaval.

But before you change everything again, be as sure as you can that this time it's for keeps.

If it is, commit yourselves to a new life together and stop all the confusion. Your marriage will need some work on it, but I'm sure it'll be worth it.

———

Q. My wife left me recently for another man. I still can't believe it. I suppose I'll get over it some day, but it's hit me very hard.

The thing is, she says we can get a quick divorce if I accuse her of adultery. But I'm not the one who wants a divorce - she is. My feeling is that she might tire of the other man and come back to me, if we remain married.

A. This must be a real nightmare for you.

The likelihood is, I'm afraid, that your wife has gone for good. But of course it's possible she just may come back, although I wouldn't want to raise your hopes.

However, there's absolutely no reason why you should be rushed into a divorce you don't want. Tell her you'll consider it, if she and her man are still happy together in two years time.

Infertility

This is a problem that affects more than one couple in seven who are trying for a child. It can cause terrible anguish, even though nowadays there is more help available than ever before.

Q. My husband and I have been trying for a baby for two years. We've both been for tests and were told everything was fine. But it has become a constant worry. I feel anxious for fourteen days before my period and then get depressed when it comes.

I'm 25 and don't want to have to go in for IVF or anything complicated. Please help. This has taken over our lives.

A. You're doing yourself no favours by allowing your natural desire for a baby to become an obsession. You're getting anxious and depressed and I bet your husband is suffering too.

But take a look at the facts:

* Tests have shown there's nothing wrong
* You're only 25

Loads of women delay their pregnancies until their thirties or even forties.

Take a deep breath and tell yourself that you have plenty of time. Also ring Issue - this is a support group for people who are trying to conceive - on: 021-344-4414.

Shyness and Loneliness

While most readers are worried about their sex problems, or their affairs, or their relationships, we agony aunts can never forget the large numbers of lonely people amongst our readers. In fact, I don't think I'm exaggerating when I say that I could fill my twice weekly columns, every week, with the letters I receive from shy and lonely people.

The trouble is that solving these problems takes enormous effort and courage. Often folk are afraid of failure, which is understandable. But one thing is certain - no-one cures their isolation by sitting at home and hoping that someone else will come visiting or take charge. Life isn't like that.

Q. I'm a 32 year old, shy man. I'm also a dead keen biker and I'd dearly love to meet a girl who could share my interests.

The trouble is that all the females I meet seem to belong to someone else.

I've tried joining a dating agency, but when I saw their brochure, all the pictures were of clean, smartly dressed people and I didn't think I would stand a chance with my leathers and long hair. Can you help?

A. You don't want ANY girl, do you? You want one who will join in the activities you like best.

No one is squeaky clean when they've just ridden 50 miles on the open road, but there are plenty of women who really go for hunky, macho men with leathers and powerful machines.

I bet some of your mates have got nice girlfriends. So why not have a chat with some of these ladies. Explain that you're bored with the girls you know and tell them you're on the look-out for a girl who'll love your bike as well as you.

Women adore matchmaking, so I expect you'll soon be spoilt for choice.

If this doesn't work, place an ad in a bikers' magazine. Try something like: "Biker seeks life-time female pillion passenger. Bring your own leathers and sense of humour".

Let me know how you get on.

———————

Q. *I'm 16 and have bad breath. I suck mints and use mouth washes, but nothing seems to help. It's especially bad in the mornings.*

A. Most people's breath isn't that sweet first thing in the morning. Brushing the teeth thoroughly generally puts things right. It's actually quite common for youngsters of your age to IMAGINE they have bad breath. But visit your dentist to make sure you have no dental problems.

Q. I've got long, red lines down my face and cheeks and nose. I suppose it's some sort of skin disease. I'm a man of 50 and this has turned me into a recluse. Im too shy to go to the doctor. Please help.

A. Please pluck up courage and go to the doctor. That's the only way you'll get help. I can't bear the thought of you having such a lonely time, when the answer might be as simple as a tube of ointment. Ring the surgery - the next fifty years could be much more fun than the last.

———

Q. I'm a very shy, single man, but recently I've begun to have very nice dreams about a girl who works at the same place as me.

She is single and quite quiet. Do you think she dreams about me too?

A. Maybe and maybe not. But it's quite clear that you'd like to get to know her better. Try inviting her for a cup of tea in the canteen, or for a drink after work.

There are lots of shy people who end up married with families. But at some point they all had to make that vital first move. Give it a try!

———————

Q. *I'm a single mum of 22 and I feel very lonely stuck in the house all the time. I'd really like to have a pen-pal, preferably in the Army. Can you help?*

A. *Soldier Magazine* accepts pen-pal requests from civilians as well as from Army personnel.

To place a personal ad in the magazine, all you have to do is to write a brief description of yourself in not more than thirty words, then post it, along with a cheque for £11.75, to: Soldier Magazine, Ordnance Road, Aldershot, Hants, GU11 2DU.

Remember to enclose an address and/or telephone number. This is just for administrative purposes and will NOT be printed in the magazine. Any replies to your ad will be sent on to you at home.

Q. *I'm a shy woman of 24. I have no real friends and have never had a boyfriend. Please don't suggest I join a club - I couldn't. But is there anything else that could help me?*

A. **There is! There's a marvellous sound cassette called** *Don't be Shy!* **which has helped countless people like you. It costs £8.50 (including postage and packing) from: Lifeskills, Bowman House, 6 Billetfield, Taunton, TA1 3NN.**

———

Q. *All my mates think I'm a fit and macho kind of a guy. But since my girlfriend walked out on me six months ago, I've been a right wimp.*

I cry in the evenings when I'm alone. I don't think I'll ever get over the pain of losing her.

What can I do to forget her?

A. **I'll bet you were told as a child that big boys don't cry. Well, it's rubbish. Crying is the best way to get over these terrible feelings.**

You need more time, that's all. Losing your girlfriend has been like a bereavement. You're entitled to feel lousy and you're definitely NOT a wimp.

Soon you'll begin to feel better about life. Try writing a list of everything you DIDN'T like about your girlfriend. That might help you to get over her. Also make sure that you start going out again with friends - even just one night a week. You'll soon realise how valued you are as a mate, which will make you feel better and eventually ready for another romance.

————————

Q. *I'm a divorced woman of 38. It's taken me a while to get myself out and about again as I'm so shy, but I took up ballroom dancing and met lots of new people. I've also had one or two dates.*

Now I've met a man who's six years younger than me. He seems attracted to me and has asked me out several times. So far I've refused, as I don't want people to laugh at me. Also I realise that I really like him - very much - so if he dropped me after a few dates because I'm too old, I think I'd die.

A. No you wouldn't. You've come through an unhappy divorce and you've coped marvellously. So even if this relationship comes to nothing, I'm sure you'll be able to deal with it.

But why should it go wrong? And if it does, maybe it will be YOU who decides that things aren't working - not him.

You're now leading a new life with fresh rules and different friends. It doesn't matter a jot if a man is a little younger than you. You fancy him, so go for it. I bet you'll be glad you did.

———

Q. *I'm not good with people. I've always been a bit of a loner I suppose. But next week it's my 25th birthday, and I'm beginning to realise that, if I don't make some sort of effort, I might always be alone.*

I'm epileptic - although I haven't had a fit for years - and I think that's held me back. I tend to feel people will think I'm odd in some way. Please can you advise me how to change my life for the better.

A. Probably it'll start changing anyway, without any help from me, simply because you've started thinking more positively.

But can I suggest an organisation that could help you. It's called Outsiders, and it's for people who are shy, feel isolated, or have some kind of disability. They have a club magazine as well as social events and computer matching, so you can choose your level of involvement. Do give it a try. Send a large stamped addressed envelope to: Outsiders, PO BOX 4ZB, London, W1A 4ZB.

———

Q. *I love women - the sight of them, the feel, the smell and the taste.*

But once I get to know a lady fully, my interest disappears. Women can't understand that, and one or two of them have been hurt because they thought I would settle down with them.

But I don't under any circumstances want a live-in relationship. That's just the way I'm built.

A. Many men would think you've got it made. You're clearly a success with women and have known plenty of them.

But before you pat yourself on the back, let me remind you that women are less likely to fall into your arms, or your bed, in twenty years from now. Are you prepared for a solitary old age?

I sense you're already a lonely man. Otherwise why would you have written? You've got some re-thinking to do, but it's up to YOU whether or not you do it!

———

Q. I work beside a quiet, shy lady who is five years older than me. She's got lovely blonde hair and a nice smile, but she's got a slight handicap and for that reason has never had a boyfriend. I know because she told me. I think I'm attracted to her because I'm quite shy myself.

I'd like to take her to see a film. But I'm worried that if I try anything on, she'll scream or get upset. However I worry too that if I DON'T try anything, she'll be insulted. It's difficult to know how to behave.

A. Well, for heaven's sake take things slowly. If you make a grab at her breasts or her naughty bits as soon as you get into the cinema, you'll probably terrify her.

Try to treat this woman with the same amount of restraint and respect that you've always done at work. If you feel confident enough to move things on a bit, then restrict yourself to holding her hand and maybe enjoying a good night kiss. If she agrees to go out again, you'll know that she's interested in taking things further in time.

BUT DON'T RUSH IT!

Q. I'm 23. For a year I've had spots on my testicles. I daren't make love to my girl in case she catches something. I've always been shy and am far too embarrassed to see my doctor.

A. You've probably got a rash through getting sweaty while you've been playing sports. But the only person who can sort this out is your doc. Please make an appointment. You've probably been worrying unnecessarily all this year. Isn't it time you took some sensible action?

Q. I'm 18 and skinny, with practically no boobs at all. This makes me very self-conscious. I'm also desperately shy and don't go out often. Last night I DID go out with some friends and a boy I know said I'd got breasts like bee-stings.

Now I'm determined to have plastic surgery, whatever it costs. My bust, or lack of it, is ruining my life. How can I go about it? I'm not sure my GP will be helpful.

A. Hang on a minute. Plenty of top models have hardly any curves at all, and they do all right!

But if you're really serious, whatever you do, don't answer any glossy cosmetic surgery ads. There are plenty of cowboy clinics around and doctors doing operations who shouldn't be let loose on animals, let alone people.

Instead contact the British Association for Aesthetic Plastic Surgery - BAAPS for short. All their surgeons are highly qualified and you'll be able to trust whatever advice you're given. Write enclosing a stamped addressed envelope to: BAAPS, Royal College of Surgeons, 35-43 Lincoln's Inn Fields, London, W2A 3PN.

Q. I'm 19 and have suffered from a very spotty skin since I was 14. My mum says I'll grow out of it, but I've got to the stage where I don't want to go out.

I've wasted lots of money on every sort of remedy at the chemist, but nothing seems to help.

Please don't think I'm making a fuss about nothing - I'm quite desperate.

A. I DON'T think you're making a fuss about nothing. Being spotty is murder - and I remember it well.

You need to try a long-term course of treatment. Go to your doctor and talk to him about antibiotics or Retin A. Either of these treatments have to be kept up for months.

Also there's a support group for people like you whose skin complaints are getting them down. For further details send a stamped addressed envelope to:- The Acne Support Group, 16 Dufour's Place, Broadwick St., London, W1V 1FE.

Q. I was lonely after I was divorced so I started writing to various women through a pen-pal magazine.

To cut a long story short, I asked a lady in the Far East to marry me and she accepted. But since the day we married she has never lived with me, we have never had sex and she has never looked after me in any way.

I have tried to be a good husband and have sent money to her family whenever she's asked me to, but I get no thanks for it.

Quite honestly I now believe she used me to get to this country and I wish I'd never married her. I want to get a divorce, but I'm worried about legal fees and what I may have to pay her.

A. Some marriages with unlikely beginnings like yours turn out extremely well. But you're living a charade. This is not a marriage and never has been.

Go along to your local Citizens' Advice Bureau. They'll help you to find legal help which you can afford.

Q. Although I'm happily married, I became very friendly with a workman during the summer. All we did was talk, but I looked forward to seeing him every day. Part of me wanted things to get more serious, but they didn't. Then his job finished and he disappeared.

Do you think he cares for me? He hasn't tried to get in touch, though he knows where I live. I feel so lonely without him. What can I do?

A. You say you're happily married. But you don't sound it.

I'm sure you signalled to the workman that you were interested in a relationship. Sensibly he didn't take you up on it - perhaps he's married himself. But he filled some kind of emotional gap in your life. Why isn't your husband filling it I wonder? Perhaps he's too busy. But unless he gives you some more attention, I fear you'll wander off with somebody else one day.

Try to spend more time with your husband. Take up a joint hobby. When your life seems fuller again, you'll forget your fancy for the workman.

Q. I've got a lot of excess hair on my face and body. It makes me very fed up. In fact I seem to be becoming more and more of a recluse as each year goes by.

I'd like to break out of all this unhappiness and go on holiday next year, but I look so disgusting undressed, I don't think I'll be able to go. What can I do?

A. Believe me, a lot of women think they are hairier than they are. They become obsessed with it, while other people don't even notice there's a problem.

But there's help at hand in the shape of an excellent book called *Hair Today, Gone Tomorrow*. It's by Anita Bradbury, and is available by mail order, price £6.99, from:- Thorsons Mail Order, Collins, PO Box Glasgow G40.

———————

Q. I'm 20 and there's this girl I'd love to take out, but I'm too shy to ask. She works in a canteen where I go sometimes, but I can't bring myself to speak to her.

A. I bet she thinks you're a refreshing change from all the lads who make suggestive comments to her while she's dishing out the chips.

Next time you're in the canteen keep going back for more cups of tea until you pluck up the courage to say, "I wonder if you'd like to have a drink with me one evening."

I hope she'll say yes, but if she doesn't, at least you'll have got a bit of practice!

———————

Q. *I'm a lonely widower and I'm friendly with a divorcee some years younger than myself. She lives in a council house and has three children, but I have my own home and feel that I could give her a better life. I go round once a week for a meal, but I want much more. How can I tell her?*

A. I fear if you suddenly come out with a declaration of undying love you may put her off. So gradually increase the number of times you see her. That way you can build up to the proposal you have in mind.

Q. My problem is that I fancy my next door neighbour.

I'm 30 and single and I think she must be in her early forties. She's been separated from her husband for more than three years and I don't think she has any other man in her life.

I say hello to her from time to time, but I'm too shy to do more. I only wish I could get to know her better - first as a friend and then in a romantic way. What should I do?

A. Haven't you seen those TV coffee ads? Mind you, they do make everything look rather too simple, don't they?

You're quite right to think in terms of friendship first, and I cannot see any reason why this woman would not be glad of a companionable, male next door neighbour. Perhaps you could start by inviting her in for coffee. Then ask her advice about re-decorating your kitchen, buying new curtains, or anything else you can think of.

You'll soon see if she's giving out friendly signals, or whether, for some reason, she wants to be left alone.

But one thing is certain, this will never be the romance of the century if you don't pluck up courage to make a move.

———————

Q. I've raised my son for four years since his mum walked out on us when he was only five months old.

I don't regret it, but I am lonely for a woman's love.

Where I live on the outskirts of Glasgow, there seem to be organised groups for mums on their own, but nothing for dads.

I've tried singles clubs, but money is tight. What can I do?

A. Your son will soon be at school, so strike up conversations with the other folk at the school gates. That way you'll begin to extend your circle of friends in general. Also put a notice in your local newsagent inviting single mums and dads to coffee. This needn't cost much. Finally join Gingerbread - a great organisation for single parents. For further information call 071-240-0953.

Q. I'm 14 and have awful dark circles under my eyes. They're ruining my life and I won't go out because of them. Please could you recommend something that would cover them up?

A. I certainly can! There's an excellent small firm that produces great camouflage make-up. I'm sure they'd be able to help you. You can obtain colour samples, which will cost you £1.50 and then, when you've selected the shade that suits you, order a larger quantity. Send your cheque to: Thomas Blake, Byre House, Fearby, near Masham, North Yorkshire, HG4 4NF.

––––––––––

Q. I'm attractive and have a good body, but I've been on my own for four years. My marriage ended after my husband had an affair. I then had one or two silly flings before deciding that I was better off on my own. I've now got my act together, but don't want to be alone for ever.

A. More people should have some time to themselves after a divorce. It's understandable that you got involved in a few unsuitable relationships. Many divorced people do the same.

But stepping back from all that was mature and quite unusual. And I'm sure you've learned a lot about yourself in the period you've been entirely alone.

You obviously now have a great deal to offer a new relationship. And I bet when you least expect it, the right man will walk into your life.

———

Q. I'm a 40 year old divorcee. I've got a good number of women friends, but sometimes I ache for a man to hold again.

There's a man across the road who's also divorced. He seems shy. Do you think I could ask HIM out?

A. Why not. It's strange that, although women have achieved so much equality, we're still nervous to approach a guy in this way. Still, faint heart never won fair gentleman!

Q. Last summer I met a man who was getting over a love affair. He was sad for a while, but as we got closer he became much happier.

I really trusted him and, at 24, fell in love for the first time. Then, on New Year's Eve, he told me he had rung the girl he used to live with and they had decided to get back together. I couldn't believe it. I thought I would die from the pain.

He still pops round every week. He says he wants to stay friends. He's also told me that things aren't great between the two of them. Do you think he might come back to me?

I tried to give him everything - yet I'm the one who's alone. It's just not fair.

A. I couldn't agree more - it ISN'T fair. But that doesn't alter anything.
We'll never know what the attraction is between the two of them. Perhaps it will last - perhaps not. But you must stop torturing yourself.

Write him a note wishing him well, but saying that it's too painful to see him any more. Then stick to it.

I know this will be agony, but he might miss you enough to come back - I hope so.

But if he doesn't, then get out and about with your old friends. At least that way you'll keep your self-respect and someone as nice as you isn't going to be alone for long.

———————

Q. I need help. I'm 14 and feel that all my classmates are calling me names and saying horrid things about me. I know this is all in my mind, but I'm terrified of losing all my friends through having these strange thoughts.

My parents just think I'm being stupid. But my sister says that what I'm going through is all part of growing up.

Sometimes though I think I'll feel like this for the rest of my life. I even feel like killing myself some days.

A. Please don't do that. It would be a terrible waste. The chances are that you're going to feel much better very soon. More people than you can imagine have had odd feelings and depressive thoughts at your age and most of them have grown up just fine.

Gather your friends about you and invite them home to listen to some records, or meet up with them in town on Saturdays. Lots of them will be experiencing strange and horrid feelings too.

But in addition I think you should pay a visit to your GP and talk to him. You could also seek out a sympathetic teacher to talk to. And don't forget the Samaritans are experts at dealing with teenage depression.

I know from experience how miserable the teens can be. Just hold on - it will pass.

Abortion

I find letters about abortion amongst the hardest to answer.

Even these days with contraception readily available, people make mistakes, and then they have to face up to the abortion issue.

Sometimes my readers are young and frightened of their parents' anger. Sometimes they're married and can't cope with any more children. Then others feel they have no option but to go for a termination because no-one will help them. This frequently happens when a woman has believed herself to be in a good and stable relationship, but then learns that her bloke has no intention of making their romance permanent, or of being a parent.

Whatever the reasons, abortion is a heart-breaking option. And, unfortunately, the troubled feelings that many men and women suffer AFTER a termination can plague them for years.

SEXUAL QUESTIONS AND ANSWERS

Q. *I went out with a boy for ten months and started to think he was going to be a permanent fixture in my life. I truly loved him.*

Then, six months ago, I got pregnant. I was on the Pill, but had had a tummy upset and so it didn't work. Naturally I thought my boyfriend would stand by me and I even thought we might marry.

Instead my boyfriend made me have an abortion and shortly afterwards, he dumped me.

I loved him so much, I would have done anything to have kept his baby. If I had known he was going to finish with me anyway, I'd definitely not have had the abortion.

I am so confused. I still love him, but I can see he's treated me very badly.

I cry for my baby every day. Please help. I am so sad, I feel I can't go on.

A. I'm sure this is the worst thing that has ever happened to you. It's particularly unfair since getting pregnant was not your fault at all.

I know that at the moment you feel you would have done anything to keep the baby, but in time you may come to feel differently. Your ex-boyfriend is spineless and cruel. Would you really have wanted the child of a man like that?

Right now though we must get you some proper help for the depression you're suffering at the loss of your child. Though it won't make you feel better instantly, you should try to realise that your feelings are entirely understandable. Abortion is an appalling trauma for many women and it can take ages to get over it.

It's worse for you as you are also mourning the end of what had seemed to be a promising relationship.

You need to talk to someone who understands what you're going through. So please contact The Post Abortion Counselling Service on 071-221-9631. They have to make a charge, I'm afraid, but it is calculated according to your situation. I'm sure that they will help you to get over your terrible sadness.

Q. I got this girl pregnant. We hardly knew each other and, to be quite honest, I didn't even like her very much. But when we discovered the baby was on the way, I felt I must offer to marry her. I thought it was the only decent thing to do.

Instead, she had a termination, saying it was nothing to do with me. This really upset me because I'm totally opposed to abortion.

Now, four months later, she's got in touch with me and said she and her mother think I should marry her after all. Do you think I have to?

A. No, I certainly do not. In fact I think the idea is crazy. You'll never be able to forgive her for aborting your child. Also you say you never liked her much - well, I should think you like her a lot less now.

Don't give in to this pressure. Tell the girl and her mother that, as far as you're concerned, the whole sorry issue is finished for good.

Q. My boyfriend wants to marry me. I really love him and he's kind, considerate and a romantic lover.

But should I tell him the secret no-one else knows - that I had an abortion five years ago?

I'm afraid that he might be shocked and it could turn him against me.

A. Unfortunately more than one in five pregnancies are terminated these days, so there are now well over a million British women with the same "secret" as yourself.

I can't tell you what to do. All I can say is that the best marriages thrive on shared secrets and absolute honesty.

However if your man has very strong religious or moral objections to abortion, he may find it hard to deal with the truth. If this is the case you might confide in someone else - like a minister, priest or close relative. I feel that after all this time you probably need to tell someone, even if it's not your husband-to-be.

Mothers and Aunties

Mothers are a surprisingly big topic in my post bag. There are women longing to be mothers, there are folk of both sexes who don't get on with their mothers and sometimes I even get letters about cruel ones.

Letters about aunties also find their way to me - but these are usually about sex. There seem to be a lot of trendy, well preserved aunties around who are keen to initiate their nephews into sex. Before I did this job I never knew aunties could be so randy!

But most of the letters I get in this group are from young readers who tell me how UNREASON-ABLE their mothers are. This is usually when the poor mums are just doing their best to keep their teenager safe from harm.

Q. *I'm 15 but my mates reckon I look 21 as I'm tall and well-built. I want to get my ear pierced so I can wear a ring in it. I reckon this would look great - lots of my mates have done it already. Unfortunately my mum is dead against it and says I'll look "poofy." Could I get it done without her permission?*

A. **Legally you're under-age and anyone who pierced your ear without your parents' consent could be in trouble with the law. So you'd be better to try gentle persuasion. Get your mates who have had their ears pierced to keep dropping by your house. When your mum realises they're just nice, ordinary, typical teenagers, she may let you have your way.**

———

Q. *I hate to say this but my husband is a real mummy's boy. We married three months ago and ever since then his mum has rung up every Saturday to ask him to put up shelves or mend a gate, or something. He moans about it, but he always goes. It's getting so that I'm spending most of my weekends alone. Sometimes I wonder if she's trying to pretend that we're not married.*

SEXUAL QUESTIONS AND ANSWERS

A. You've hit the nail right on the head! She wants life as it was before. And you're both playing into her hands, because your husband goes to her - alone.

Try getting to the phone first. Then when she asks for your husband to come over on a Saturday, tell her that you have something arranged on that day. Offer her an evening instead. But when the evening arrives, you go too! It doesn't matter if you can't bear the thought - you're fighting for your future.

While your husband puts up the shelf, talk to her about her life, or about your husband when he was small. That way she can't pretend you don't exist. And hopefully her requests for visits will start to dwindle.

———————

Q. *My mum spent the last thirty years raising my sister, my brother and me. Now I feel she deserves some time to herself. But my brother is always asking her to baby-sit, including every Saturday night. Mum's too nice to say no. What can I do to change things?*

A. First of all make sure that your mum really does feel hard done by. It may be that she loves baby-sitting and can't get enough of it. But if she is sick of being taken for granted, she should tell your brother that she has other plans for the next few Saturdays. If she's too shy to do this, then you and your sister must pluck up courage and tell your brother how selfish he's being.

Q. My mother is an interfering, sarcastic woman. I often pay some of her bills or give her the odd thirty quid, because she moans about being hard-up. But she always finds money for bingo, drink and cigarettes. I phone her when I can, but she's so nasty, I often end the conversation in tears.

My wonderful husband hates to see me upset by her. We are still very much in love after eleven years of marriage. But he and my mother don't get on at all. And I feel torn in two. I keep thinking I should try harder. After all you only have one mum, don't you? But she is a very nasty minded person. And I'm worried she'll come between me and my husband.

A. You want to rule your mother out of your life. But you feel guilty, so you're asking me to tell you it's OK.

Well, go ahead. Drop her out of sight. Your marriage is much more important. But then you CHOSE your husband, didn't you? Whereas your mother was selected for you in the lottery of life. And not everybody gets a winner, I'm afraid.

———

Q. I've discovered that my mother is behaving very strangely. She lives round the corner from quite a posh boys' school and I hear she's started inviting some of the older ones into the house.

I'm especially worried because recently she's begun to dress in the latest teenage fashions and I'm terribly afraid she may actually be having sex with these boys.

She was depressed after my dad died and had a lot of pills from the doctor, but now she's become very lively and happy. In fact she stays up half the night watching videos and says she's never tired. Do you think I should interfere?

A. I hope none of the boys is under sixteen, or your mother could end up in serious trouble. From what you say, I think she's probably ill. It's not natural for someone to suddenly stop grieving and become energetic and wakeful. In fact I think there's a real possibility that she may suddenly change again from being lively and outrageous to being suicidal. So please tell her doctor what you've told me.

———————

Q. I am almost 16. I've had three girlfriends, but I don't know much about sex.

I have an auntie I get on very well with. I go to stay with her when my mum, who's divorced, goes out with her boyfriend. Anyway last week I was talking about sex with my aunt, when she laughed and said that, as soon as I'm sixteen, she'll be happy to teach me all I need to know.

She's a very attractive woman of about thirty-five with big breasts, and partly I can't help feeling really excited about going to bed with her.

But I'm scared too. And the other thing is, could I get her pregnant?

SEXUAL QUESTIONS AND ANSWERS

A. NO-ONE knows much about sex when they're 15 - so you're no different from anybody else. Please take that fact on board.

But sex is something that should be learned in a happy, loving way with someone you care about. And preferably someone in your own age group.

Of course I can well understand your excitement. After all many young boys dream of losing their virginity to an older, more experienced woman. And - by the way - many older women have fantasies about schooling young gents in the art of love.

But this lady is your AUNT. It would be VERY seedy to have sex with her. Also, it could cause all sorts of family rows and she might prove difficult when you decide to practise what she's taught you with a much younger girl.

Don't do it. I'm sure in the end you'd regret it. And - yes - it's quite possible you could get her pregnant. What a mess THAT would be.

Q. I couldn't wait to grow up and marry and have babies. Now I've done all these things, I'm horrified at how dull I've become. I'm not even very interested in sex.

A. Don't worry, you need a bit of time to yourself, that's all. You've forgotten how to be a person in your own right rather than a mum.

Look after a friend's children for a few hours a week in exchange for a free day yourself. Then get out and enjoy your own company. Go shopping, or visit the library. Have a cup of coffee in a nice café and read a magazine. You could even go to the cinema - that's great fun in the afternoon. Make sure you treat yourself to a tub of popcorn and a fizzy drink!

Whatever you do, enjoy it - and relish the fact that you're out alone without a toddler's sticky fingers dragging on your skirt all the time.

I'm sure when you get home your babes will seem the most enchanting kids in the world. And I bet you'll rediscover your sex drive too, before long.

I never hear what happens to many of the people who write to me, although I often wonder about them. But from time to time someone writes a really nice thank-you letter in response to one of my replies. That can be very cheering. Here's one of my favourites.

Q. *Some time ago I was having a lot of trouble with my relationships and also finding it difficult to see my little boy. So I wrote to you. Your reply helped me a lot and since then I've tried to do some of the things you suggested.*

I wouldn't say everything is wonderful now, but it's certainly better. I'd like to send you some flowers, but money is very tight, so instead I'm sending you a photograph of some daffodils as they will last longer than any bouquet.

Christine Webber - TV personality, romantic novelist and Britain's most outspoken agony aunt - has recorded advice lines especially for her readers. Call her now for confidential advice on:

ERECTION PROBLEMS 0891-666-778

MASTURBATION FOR MEN 0891-666-779

MASTURBATION FOR WOMEN 0891-666-780

ORAL SEX FOR MEN 0891-666-781

ORAL SEX FOR WOMEN 0891-666-782

REACHING ORGASM (WOMEN) 0891-666-783

FOUR WAYS TO PLEASE A MAN 0891-666-784

FOUR WAYS TO PLEASE A WOMAN .. 0891-666-785

These advice lines are only available in the UK. Calls cost 39 pence per minute cheap rate and 49 pence per minute at all other times.

A product of TIM Ltd., 4 Selsdon Way, London, E14 9GL (details correct at time of publication).